TRADING THE FUNDAMENTALS

THE TRADER'S COMPLETE GUIDE TO INTERPRETING ECONOMIC INDICATORS & MONETARY POLICY

MICHAEL P. NIEMIRA
GERALD F. ZUKOWSKI

PROBUS PUBLISHING COMPANY
Chicago, Illinois
Cambridge, England

Printed in the United States of America

BB

2 3 4 5 6 7 8 9 0

Dedicated To

Kathleen, Alexis, Sarah, and Keith
GFZ

Andrew
MPN

Table of Contents

List of Figures

Preface

Investors today are more savvy than ever about the interaction of the economy and monetary policy. News reporting is faster, more detailed, and more analytical; investors are compelled to understand more thoroughly the intricacies of economic data and the conduct of monetary policy. It is the intent of this book to help fill in and expand investors' understanding of the fundamentals which ultimately drive the financial markets.

We would like to thank Robert Bretz, Jeremy Gluck, Samuel Kahan, and Martin Mauro for their helpful comments and suggestions on various sections of this book.

We would also like to acknowledge Pamela van Giessen and the staff of Probus Publishing for their understanding and support along the way. Of course, all remaining errors and omissions are our own.

Section 1

Analyzing Business Conditions

Chapter 1

Understanding Economic Indicators

Overview

Every economic indicator has a story to tell. The role of the trader (dealer) of fixed-income instruments, stocks, options, futures, and foreign currency is to determine quickly that story and the significance of a move in the indicator. In most cases, the market reaction to an economic news report is partly determined by: (1) the market consensus forecast, (2) how significant data revisions are in previous periods, (3) the reliability and comprehensiveness of an economic indicator, and (4) how important the indicator is thought to be to policy makers. In a broad sense, the fixed-income and exchange rate markets tend to react more directly to the economic news than the stock market, which is also dependent on specific company and industry fundamentals. The fixed-income markets are concerned with the pace of economic growth and inflation; the foreign exchange markets tend to worry about the pace of economic growth, inflation, and foreign trade imbalances; the stock market is interested in earnings, which are driven by economic growth and the asset allocation implications from changes in interest rates.

Numerous surveys of the major economic indicator forecasts exist, and there is a good deal of overlap in who participates in the forecast surveys. Most major firms participate in most of the consensus surveys. Some of the more widely followed consensus takers are: Bloomberg Business News, Dow-Jones Capital Markets, Knight-Ridder Financial News, Market News Service,

Money Market Services, MCM's MoneyWatch, and Technical Data Corporation.

Some economic indicators tend to have a greater market impact than other series because of their breadth in coverage, depth of detail, and their timeliness. In most cases, the market's technical indicators along with global political factors play a role in determining how significant a market reaction will be and whether the financial market reaction is "as expected" or just the reverse. As a rough guide to how the financial markets react to the economic news, Figure 1–1 below illustrates the "normal" market reaction.

FIGURE 1–1 Assessing Financial Market Impact of Economic News

Market	Stronger/Larger than Expected		Weaker/Lower than Expected	
	Business Conditions	Inflation	Business Conditions	Inflation
Fixed Income (prices)	↓	↓	↑	↑
U.S. Equity (prices)	↑	↓	↓	↑
Foreign Exchange (dollar)	↑	↑	↓	↓

Economic Indicators over the Business Cycle

It is our contention that the best way for a trader or any investor to understand the economic indicators and potentially how policy makers will react to the information is to use a business cycle framework. A *business cycle* is simply the way that growth takes place. *Recessions* are triggered when imbalances in the cost-price-profit relationship occur, which often are caused by a shock or cumulative excess in the economy. *Recoveries* are phases of the cycle delineated from the economy's low point or trough until the economy recaptures its lost output. *Expansions* are cyclical phases marked by when the economy expands beyond its prior cyclical high. But expansions also include periods of accelerating and decelerating growth, which are called *growth cycles* (also popularly known as *mini-cycles* or *growth rate cycles*). The National Bureau of Economic Research, which is the arbiter of the official business-cycle turning point dates, also produces a growth cycle chronology, which is maintained by Columbia University's Center for International Business Cycle Research. Although it is important to make the conceptual distinction between mini-cycle phases of an expansion, it is rather difficult to statistically delineate those periods in most economic series without relying on sophisticated methods. The best advice is to use the rules of thumb for each indicator. If the pattern of change in an economic indicator is consistent with below average gains for expansions, then it is quite likely that the economy is in a growth slowdown. Importantly, a characteristic of a growth rate slowdown within an economic expansion is a tendency for the pace of inflation to moderate as well. Hence, the inflation/growth nexus is a useful—though not foolproof—checkpoint for identifying this cycle phase, which in many cases will result in lower long-term interest rates. Moreover, during the postwar period, 82 percent of all growth cycle peaks were a precursor to a business cycle recession.

Not surprisingly, a huge body of literature has developed that proves economic indicators behave differently during recessions and expansions. Most recently, our research along with studies done at the Federal Reserve Board and the Federal Reserve Bank of Dallas[1] suggests that it is not sufficient to distinguish only between recessions and contractions. In analyzing the performance of the economy based on an economic indicator, we describe the fluctuation of the indicator for each of its three cyclical phases: (1) the recession (or, contraction), (2) the recovery or transition period between the cyclical trough and when the economy returns to its previous peak, and (3) the expansion. These cycle phases are captured in Figure 1–2, which shows the typical cyclical pattern for industrial production. But as always

---

1   See: Daniel E. Sichel, "Inventories and the Three Phases of the Business Cycle," manuscript, Federal Reserve Board, August 1992. Also see: Kenneth M. Emery and Evan F. Koenig, "Forecasting Turning Points: Is a Two-State Characterization of the Business Cycle Appropriate?" Research Paper, Federal Reserve Bank of Dallas, September 1992.

FIGURE 1–2 Phases of the Business Cycle
Industrial Production Index

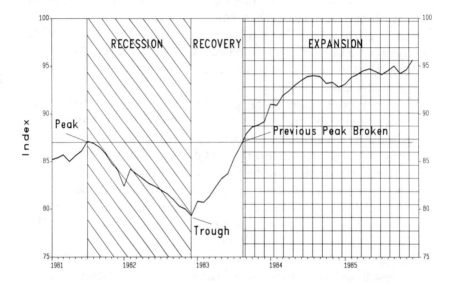

not every business cycle or economic series will follow its typical pattern.

The statistical distinction between recovery and expansion is not trivial—the performance of an economic indicator is usually very different for each of these periods. The trader/investor is presented with a table for each indicator that is divided into those three types of growth rate environments to judge not only the strength of the change, but also the likely category to which it belongs. As a general rule, growth is the strongest during the recovery as economic activity attempts to recoup lost momentum. But, on average, that period also tends to have a duration that is slightly less than the length of the recession. Not surprisingly, the expansion has the longest duration—though prior to World War II, recessions tended to be longer than during the post-WWII period while expansions tended to be shorter. The federal government's counter-cyclical fiscal policy was a key reason for longer expansions than recessions during the postwar period. However, in the 1990s the federal government's ability to implement counter-cyclical policy was severely weakened by its large federal budget deficits, which ultimately may shorten future expansions. In assessing the duration of future business cycles, it is important to keep an eye on longer term fundamentals as well.

Although a technical discussion of each indicator is presented in isolation, the trader (helped a bit by the firm's economists and astute reporters) and investors should generally view each indicator as a mosaic. No single indicator provides the whole picture but only a piece of it and even that could be blurred by data deficiencies. A trader, in particular, is handicapped if he or she reacts to an economic indicator report without understanding what it measures, how it is measured, its limitations, and its relationship to other economic measures.

Finally, there is no clearer reflection of the power and importance of these economic news reports than in witnessing how the information is guarded and who is privy to the information before the official release. Only the president of the United States through the chair of the Council of Economic Advisers (CEA) is given the full contents of a government-issued economic report prior to its official release time. Generally, the president is informed of the economic news on the evening prior to the scheduled release. In turn, the president's representative—the CEA chairperson, as a courtesy—advises the chairperson of the Federal Reserve Board of Governors about the essence of the economic report. Thus, the government's highest fiscal and monetary policy makers are privy to the information before the public is notified.

Everyone else must wait until the official release time to know the latest economic data, though the news media, which will be the first to break the news to the public, are given the major market-sensitive government economic indicators one-half hour early to facilitate that dissemination. But because they are sensitive data, the press are held in "lockup" at the various government agencies to prevent early release.

In the following pages, each economic indicator is discussed in sections that allow for easy reference. The placement of the economic indicator descriptions was based on an alphabetical listing and not on their market importance or their typical release schedule during the month. Over time, the market significance of some economic indicators has shifted, given broader global, political, and economic concerns. For example, in the early 1980s the money supply was riding high in its importance for the markets, but by the end of the 1980s this was no longer true due to the unstable short-term empirical link between money, growth, and inflation. A shift in market focus also occurred for the merchandise trade report, which was a very significant market mover in the late 1980s, but its importance dwindled as the trade gap narrowed due to the impact and market preoccupation with the 1990–91 recession. The "major" themes often determine what is important for the financial markets at any given time. If the concern is inflation, then the CPI and PPI reports take on more significance. If the concern is the dollar's impact on trade and the real economy, then the merchandise trade report is the report *de jure* and so forth.

As a general rule, the National Association of Purchasing Management's Purchasing Managers' Index is the first nationwide indicator for the prior month, followed by monthly chain store sales and car sales; and on the first Friday of the month, the employment report is released. The price indexes—the U.S. Consumer Price Index (CPI) and the producer price index (PPI) —tend to be reported late in the second or early in the third week of the month. The real gross domestic product (GDP), personal income and consumption, index of leading indicators, and factory orders reports all tend to be reported late in the month with most other economic reports in the third week of the month. In December, the U.S. federal government statistical agencies under the coordination of the Office of Management and Budget announce scheduled release dates for the upcoming year, and for the most part those dates are not changed. When a date is changed for some unforeseen reason, the statistical agency alerts data users of the change as soon as possible.

Each indicator discussion addresses several key questions, such as what it measures, why look at it, how it is used, and how the market tends to react to the data. Any market reaction discussion is only suggestive, since as previously noted external factors play a role in determining the strength and type of market reaction. Additionally, a data performance table is included with each indicator. The series performance is judged by our statistical rules of thumb for interpreting the economic indicator, which provides a quick guide to assess the strength or weakness of an indicator's change. But because all data are "noisy," a *normal high* and a *normal low* band is presented. "Normal" is defined by the average plus or minus one-half of the average absolute deviation. A wide normal band should alert the user to very high volatility in the series, which can alternatively be measured directly in the standard deviation.

Informing the Public: The Press Lockup

Jon E. Hilsenrath
Knight-Ridder Financial News
Washington, DC

When Adren Cooper first came to the Commerce Department in 1966, there was little structure to the government's release of economic data. Cooper says President Lyndon Johnson sometimes announced upbeat reports himself, in speeches. But more sleepy reports could sit on tables for hours on release dates, untouched by reporters.

Twenty-seven years later, journalists from newswires around the world crowd into the fifth-floor Commerce Department press room, scrambling to get out as many numbers as financial markets can digest. Cooper now runs these so-called lockups for Commerce.

The Commerce Department and Labor Department, both driven by fears and rumors of leaks in recent years, have taken to locking reporters into their press rooms for key reports, giving them 30 minutes to prepare stories for release.

Reporters come to these lockups armed with editors and statisticians to help put together tables, headlines and stories. Between 8 a.m. and 8:30 a.m., the door is closed behind them and their phones are disconnected from the outside world.

During more complex reports, like the 20-page unemployment report, lockup rooms can become hectic, as reporters search for nuances in the data and dozens of stat people read out numbers for tables. According to Labor Department officials, as many as 25 organizations may be present at key lockups, including representatives from French, German, English and Japanese agencies.

Still concerned about leaks of the data, both Commerce and Labor attach unusual rules to their lockups. Emergency trips to the bathroom require a government escort. When phone lines are opened at 8:29 a.m. to connect to copy desks, all conversations must be in English. And that conversation cannot concern the data until the Naval Observatory deems it is exactly 8:30 Eastern time.

In a global marketplace, releasing a few numbers just isn't simple anymore.

Chapter 2

Business Inventories and Sales

General Description

The business inventory data are collected from three sources: the manufacturing, merchant wholesalers, and retail trade reports. Inventory calculations at all levels are based on book values of merchandise held at the end of the month. (See Figure 2–1.)

Economic Indicator Information at a Glance

Market Significance	Low
Typical Release Time	10:00 AM Eastern Time Tenth Business Day
Released By	Commerce Department Census Bureau
Period Covered	Two Months Prior

The data are broken into inventories, sales, and the inventory-to-sales (I/S) ratio at each of the three levels. A breakdown is also available at each level for durable and nondurable sectors. At the time of release of the total business inventory and sales data, only the retail inventory portion is unknown. Manufacturing inventory levels and sales (also known as shipments) were available about two weeks prior, the merchant wholesaler sales and inventory component about five business days before, and the retail sales portion a month ahead of this release.

FIGURE 2–1 Business Inventories and Sales Percentage Share: End of 1992

	Inventories	Sales
Manufacturing	45%	44%
Merchant Wholesalers	25%	27%
Retail Trade	30%	29%

It would be difficult to analyze properly the inventory data without stepping back and understanding how inventory management has changed in the last decade. The level of inventories that companies now choose to hold relative to sales has dropped to historic lows. Just-in-time inventory management techniques have been adopted, and every manager on every level of business tries to keep inventories as low as possible without harming the flow of production or sales. This "micro-tracking" makes it difficult to put current inventory information into historical perspective. Leads and lags are shorter, and the data itself is not likely to suffer the extremes as in the past. Where inventories were used historically to absorb temporary shocks to demand, business inventories now play a significantly lessened role as a buffer for economic activity.

Even with this in mind, inventories and the I/S ratio still conform to a basic pattern. Inventories and the I/S ratio are lagging indicators, particularly in a cyclical context. Sales are the component that initially drive the business cycle, and drive the I/S ratio at the same time. Inventory adjustment is a lagging indicator of the falloff in sales; and in a sense, it can be considered a second step in the recessionary process, or for that matter, in a recovery. It is the initial drop in demand that initiates a recession and then restarts growth.

Analyzing the Data

With 70 percent of the inventory and 100 percent of the sales information already available, one can go into the release having a pretty good idea what will happen. That having been said, retail inventories are the most volatile component of inventories and can cause major swings.

Jumps or large drops in the I/S ratio are something to look for, but the information is more for background knowledge of the economy than something from which to derive an immediate trade. There is no rule of thumb that says, for example, that increases (decreases) in inventories or the I/S ratio are good (bad) for the fixed-income markets or bad (good) for equities. One of the reasons is the need to distinguish between unwanted and desired inventory swings. Unfortunately there is no quantitative way to ascertain this. Today, it would seem any increase in the I/S ratio would be considered unwanted, but this is taking the point too far. If business is growing, there are reasons to rebuild inventories. Maybe the inventory levels attained years ago are no longer a valid basis of comparison, but one should not expect the I/S ratio to move only in a two or three hundredths of a point range or view any increase in the inventory level or I/S ratio as bad for business in subsequent months.

One place to start to determine if a given inventory change might be positive or negative for the fixed-income or equity markets, and in so doing appraising whether it might be unwanted or desired, is to place it within its cyclical context. For example, a decline in inventories takes on a different story if it happens during a slowdown or during the latter stages of a recovery. A drop in inventories during a recession, especially early in the cycle stage, normally alludes to business wanting to reduce stocks, and in so doing production and output needs to be cut. But a decline during the recovery stage takes on a more positive light. It may be desired, initially, but over time a drop in inventories during a recovery stage can be construed as unwanted, and therefore lead to production and output gains in subsequent months.

Another way to analyze or use inventory data is to consider its potential contribution to upcoming or already released GDP estimates. Inventory data are one of the key swing sectors of the GDP accounts, and the Department of Commerce's monthly inventory data, after much massaging, is one of the sources the Bureau of Economic Analysis (BEA) uses to estimate real end of quarter inventory levels. Although one can create a fundamental, underlying story with the numbers and what that story means for economic activity, the data's potential statistical impact on a yet to be released GDP estimate can be just as important, if not more so, than any story. The GDP estimate is one of the critical releases for the market, and if the monthly inventory data point to GDP coming in significantly different than expectations, it holds important information. This angle also holds after a quarter's first estimate of GDP growth is released. The initial GDP estimate for a quarter includes an estimate for inventories in the final month of the quarter. No hard data was available at the time of the original GDP release. Sometimes the difference between the BEA's estimate and the actual inventory can be quite sizeable and result in a fairly pivotal change in the GDP estimate. Also, when it comes to translating the monthly Census Dept.'s inventory data to the GDP accounts, the phrase "there is much slip twixt cup and lip" comes immediately to mind. The linkage is loose, to say the least; and although directions are typically similar, magnitudes of change can vary significantly given the Commerce Department's adjustments for valuation and inflation. Speaking from personal experiences, many analysts have impaled themselves on swords, when a large swing in the monthly nominal inventory data failed to show up in the GDP inventory change component.

Business Inventories over the Business Cycle

Business inventories are a critical part of the business cycle, and their large swings are often masked by business cycle averages. Inventories grow faster during recessions, on average, than they do in recoveries. The recession pace of accumulation also matches the average rate of increase during expansions. But this recession average masks sharp swings as seen by the fact that both the historic high and low rate of inventory accumulation were registered in a recession. During recessions, inventories show their greatest accumulation as demand sinks and stocks pile up at the onset of a recession and their sharpest drop as business reacts swiftly to the prior unwanted accumulation. The recovery phase of the business cycle actually shows a slower average rate of inventory building than the expansion. This is because inventory building requires confidence, and it takes sustained activity to convince businesses that stockpiling goods is warranted. (See Figures 2–2a, 2–2b.)

FIGURE 2–2a Business Inventories

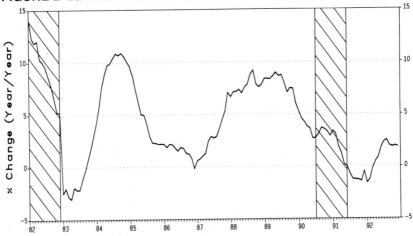

Note: Shaded areas represent business cycle recessions

FIGURE 2–2b Business Inventories
(January 1981–December 1992, Percent Change)

Period	Historic Low	Normal Bounds			Historic High	Series Characteristics		
		Normal Low	Average	Normal High		Standard Deviation	Share of Total Observations	
Recession	−0.9% in Mar 1991	−0.4 %	+0.4%	+1.2%	+7.0% in Jan 1982	1.5 pp.	24	16.7%
Recovery	−0.8% in Jan 1983	+0.1 %	+0.3%	+0.6%	+1.3% in Feb 1984	0.5 pp.	37	25.7%
Expansion	−0.7% in Dec 1986	+0.2 %	+0.4%	+0.6%	+1.3% in Oct 1987	0.4 pp.	83	57.6%

Chapter 3

Car and Truck Sales

General Description

Car and truck sales are reported individually by the manufacturers and seasonally adjusted by the Commerce Department—though the Federal Reserve also produces its own seasonally adjusted aggregate sales figures. The Commerce Department computes seasonally adjusted data for cars—both on a 10-day and a monthly basis, and those seasonal adjustment factors have became the benchmark that economists use for expressing and discussing the seasonally adjusted selling rate. The Commerce Department only provides seasonally adjusted light-domestic truck sales data on a monthly basis, although those sales figures are reported on a 10-day basis as well. Consequently, the Federal Reserve Board's 10-day light-domestic truck seasonal factors are becoming more widely accepted as the standard seasonal-adjustment method for 10-day light-truck data. Imported car sales generally are reported for the month only.

Economic Indicator Information at a Glance

Market Significance	Moderate
Typical Release Time	Third business day after the ten-day period ends
Released By	Motor vehicle manufacturers and Seasonally Adjusted by the Commerce Department
Period Covered	Prior Ten-day Period

Analyzing the Data

Car sales are a consumer and an investment good depending on the purchaser. About two-thirds of cars purchased are by consumers, and nearly the rest are sold to businesses with a tiny fraction of the market going to all levels of government. With the rise in the popularity of the mini-van and sport utility vehicles, U.S. truck sales have become a growing share of the overall motor vehicle market. Mini-vans and utility vehicles are classified as "light trucks" by the industry. In 1991 they accounted for about 40 percent of the total truck market (see Figure 3–1). The consumers' long-run preference shift to mini-vans and sport utility vehicles has resulted in a dwindling share of passenger cars being bought by the consumer. For example, over the last 25 years the consumer share of the car market peaked in September 1968 at 77.1 percent (but on trend had been around 75 percent of the market at that time) and reached an all-time low in May 1991 at 49.1 percent.

Total unit truck sales account for about one-third of total motor vehicle unit sales—about half as large as auto sales. By nominal value, truck sales accounted for 36.4 percent of the value of 1991 motor vehicle sales. Moreover, based on vehicle registrations, trucks represented a higher percentage of total motor new vehicle registrations in 1991 for the eleventh consecutive year. As a result, truck sales and production are factors that must be reckoned with in monitoring and forecasting the U.S. economy.

A telling sign of the "new" motor vehicle market is that Chrysler—once a premier passenger car manufacturer—is today primarily a truck manufacturer. Over the first half of 1992, the big three—General Motors, Ford, and Chrysler—garnered 83 percent of the truck market but only 65 percent of the car market. But competition from the U.S. "transplants" for the light truck market is growing, especially from Nissan, Toyota, and Isuzu.

Fleet demand is another issue in understanding the motor vehicle market. Fleet demand comprises two types of buyers: (1) the car rental companies and (2) company/government fleets. In 1991 *Automotive Fleet* found that fleet demand accounted for 2.6 mn. units sold, which was slightly more than 30 percent of total car sales. Fleet demand has been used by the major car manu-

FIGURE 3–1 1991 U.S. Truck Market by Segment
(Domestic and Imported Unit Sales)

Type of Vehicle	Sales
Compact pickup	982,202
Full-sized pickup	1,086,051
Mini-van	877,345
Full-sized van	308,254
Compact sports vehicle	786,546
Full-sized sport-utility	119,018
Total Light Trucks	4,159,416
Share of Total Truck Sales	95.2%
Domestic	3,446,744
Share of Light Truck Sales	82.9%
Share of Total Truck Sales	78.9%
Foreign	712,672
Total Truck Sales	4,367,752
Addendum:	
Minivan Shares of Light Trucks	21.1%
Truck Sales as a Share of Auto Sales	53.4%
Truck Sales as a Share of Total Motor Vehicle Sales	33.7%

Source: *Automotive News*

facturers as a "cushion" for their sales, since fleet sales can be booked in periods when consumer sales are particularly slow.

Motor Vehicle Sales over the Business Cycle

The Commerce Department classifies car sales as a leading indicator of the business cycle, but in recent times it has become far more coincident and far more influential as a "swing factor" in the economy. Car and truck sales have a typical-cycle pattern with the strongest gains in the recovery phase of the cycle. On average, car sales increase by 1.5 percent per month during the

FIGURE 3–2a U.S. Car and Truck Sales

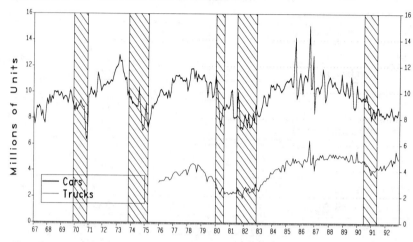

Note: Shaded areas represent business cycle recessions

FIGURE 3-2b U.S. Truck Sales
(February 1976–December 1992, Percent Change)

Period	Historic Low	Normal Bounds			Historic High	Series Characteristics	
		Normal Low	Average	Normal High		Standard Deviation	Share of Total Observations
Recession	−15.2% in Sep 1981	−5.1 %	0.7 %	6.5 %	+31.9% in Jan 1982	11.6 pp.	30	14.8%
Recovery	−13.8% in Dec 1982	−1.9 %	0.9 %	3.7 %	+12.2% in Mar 1983	5.6 pp.	59	29.1%
Expansion	−29.2% in Oct 1986	−3.6 %	0.3 %	4.2 %	+22.1% in Sep 1986	7.7 pp.	114	56.2%

FIGURE 3-2c U.S. Car Sales
(February 1976–December 1992, Percent Change)

Period	Historic Low	Normal Bounds			Historic High	Series Characteristics	
		Normal Low	Average	Normal High		Standard Deviation	Share of Total Observations
Recession	−17.8% in Oct 1981	−5.7 %	−1.0 %	3.7 %	+22.7% in Aug 1981	9.4 pp.	57	18.3%
Recovery	−7.9% in Apr 1991	−1.9 %	1.5 %	4.9 %	+44.4% in Jan 1971	6.7 pp.	83	26.7%
Expansion	−34.5% in Jan 1987	−3.9 %	0.2 %	4.3 %	+25.0% in Sep 1986	8.1 pp.	171	55.0%

recovery and then moderate to a 0.2 percent pace during the expansion. Truck sales typically increase 0.9 percent per month during the recovery and slow to a gain of 0.3 percent per month thereafter. During recessions, car sales tend to decline by 1.0 percent per month, but truck sales tend to hold up—growing at a 0.7 percent pace. That, in part, reflects a secular shift toward light trucks and away from the passenger car. (See Figures 3–2a, 3–2b, 3–2c.)

Relationship with Other Series

Car and truck sales are used directly in the Commerce Department's compilation of personal consumption data. These data also provide a window on the Census Bureau's automotive dealers retail sales. There are numerous measurement differences between unit car sales and the value of automotive dealer sales. Those differences include: (1) seasonal factors, (2) coverage (e.g., auto dealer sales include used car sales), and (3) composition (value data can change solely due to shifts in the price of cars purchased even if the overall number of units sold is unchanged.)

These unit data also are used to compute the *days' supply of unsold vehicles*—which is a widely followed industry inventory-to-sales measure. Normally, the days' supply of unsold cars runs 60–65 days—though in some months that figure tends to be higher such as in January, when it averages about 75 days while in September, the figure tends to drop to about 55 days with the start of the new model year. But excessive stock relative to demand is likely to result in a paring of production schedules and should be watched. (See Figure 3–3.)

FIGURE 3–3 Days' Supply of Unsold Domestically Produced Passenger Cars

Period	1967-92	Jan	Feb	Mar	Apr	May	Jun	Jul	Aug	Sep	Oct	Nov	Dec
Obs:	312	26	26	26	26	26	26	26	26	26	26	26	26
Average	61.8	74.6	65.2	60.7	61.3	58.0	60.6	59.8	59.5	57.8	55.7	62.3	69.0
Maximum	106.9	105.0	78.0	77.0	78.7	83.3	83.5	87.6	87.6	70.7	81.4	88.0	106.9
Minimum	35.0	54.0	51.1	43.9	47.9	44.2	46.9	44.4	48.1	35.0	36.5	36.8	45.6
Std. Dev.	12.1	12.5	6.7	8.4	8.1	9.3	10.8	11.1	8.3	9.5	12.4	14.7	14.0

Chapter 4

Construction Expenditures

General Description and Analysis of the Data

The official title of this series is "The Value of New Construction Put in Place." Its data is derived from progress reports filed by owners of a sample of construction projects throughout the 50 states and the District of Columbia. The data are valued in nominal and real dollars. The main breakdown in each is divided into private and public construction expenditures, with private construction further broken down into residential buildings and nonresidential buildings. (See Figure 4–1.)

Economic Indicator Information at a Glance

Market Significance	Low
Typical Release Time	10:00 AM Eastern Time First Business Day of the Month
Released By	Commerce Department Census Bureau
Period Covered	Two Months Prior

This is a very volatile series, both on the private and public side. It is also subject to sizeable revision. Its market significance is very limited, as financial markets utilize the housing starts statistic as a gauge of the housing market. The release's importance is primarily for analysts. The data, both on the private and public sides, are important inputs into GDP calculations;

namely, residential investment, business spending on structures, and state and local government spending.

FIGURE 4–1 Construction Expenditures*: Percentage Break-down End of 1992

Private Construction	73%
Residential Buildings	45%
Nonresidential Buildings	19%
TeleCommunications	2%
Other Private	6%
Public Construction	27%

*Nominal Dollars

Construction Expenditures over the Cycle

Month-to-month changes in construction expenditures follow the business cycle closely. They decline on average during recessions, grow strongest during the recovery, and grow more moderately during the expansion. The key is the different timing of the residential and nonresidential construction sectors. Residential construction tends to be a leading indicator of the business cycle, similar to housing starts. Nonresidential investment, however, tends to drop most noticeably only after the recession has begun, and it tends to increase after the recovery has started. These two different patterns create a seemingly "average" series. (See Figures 4–2a, 4–2b.)

FIGURE 4–2a Construction Expenditures

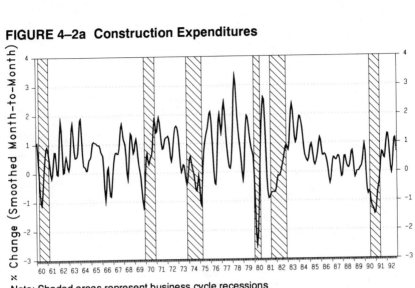

Note: Shaded areas represent business cycle recessions

FIGURE 4–2b Construction Expenditures
(February 1958–December 1992, Percent Change)

Period	Historic Low	Normal Bounds			Historic High	Series Characteristics		
		Normal Low	Average	Normal High		Standard Deviation	Share of Total Observations	
Recession	−4.8% in Feb 1975	−1.3 %	−0.4 %	0.5%	+4.4% in Jan 1975	1.8 pp.	70	16.7%
Recovery	−4.8% in Aug 1958	0.3%	1.2 %	2.1%	+8.6% in Sep 1958	1.8 pp.	104	24.8%
Expansion	−3.3% in May 1966	−0.3 %	0.5 %	1.3%	+6.6% in Jan 1964	1.6 pp.	245	58.5%

Chapter 5

Consumer Confidence Measures

General Description

Three widely followed consumer confidence measures are available from (1) the University of Michigan, (2) the Conference Board, and (3) ABC News and *Money* magazine. Over the longer run, they all move together; consumer confidence surveys serve as a reflection of national mood about the present and the degree of the consumers' hopes or dismay about the future. Sometimes the consumer worries about inflation more than unemployment, and at other times the reverse is true. But in either case, consumer confidence reflects the paramount economic concern facing the nation or the individual. Consumer confi-

Economic Indicator Information at a Glance

Market Significance	Moderate
Typical Release Time Conference Board	10:00 AM Eastern Time Last Thursday of Month
Period Covered	Current Month
Typical Release Time University of Michigan	10:00 AM Eastern Time Second Friday (1) and Last Day (2) of Month
Period Covered	First half of Current Month (1) and Full Current Month (2)
Typical Release Time ABC News/*Money* magazine	6:30 PM Eastern Time Wednesday or Thursday
Period Covered	Week ending prior Sunday

dence is far more important to the financial markets during times of national crisis or panic—such as after the 1987 stock market crash, before and during the 1991 Persian Gulf War, after oil shocks, during recessions, and so forth.

Analyzing the Data

The Conference Board survey is done by mail (using 5,000 households) while the other two surveys are telephone surveys. The ABC News/*Money* poll (which includes about 1,000 households) is the only weekly poll, though the University of Michigan survey is taken across the month and a preliminary reading is released after about two weeks into the month (when about half of their total 500 household survey is complete). All three series are reported in different forms: (1) the University of Michigan series is a net difference plus 100; that is, 100 + BETTER–WORSE, where BETTER is the share of the sample reporting better and WORSE the share reporting worse, (2) the Conference Board measure is calculated as [BETTER/(BETTER + WORSE)] and is the only series that is seasonally adjusted, and (3) the ABC News poll is simply BETTER–WORSE, and only is reported on a four-week moving average basis.

The Conference Board and University of Michigan surveys include consumer evaluations of both current and future conditions (expectations) while the ABC News poll only captures current conditions on a weekly basis. The Conference Board and University of Michigan overall consumer sentiment indexes are a weighted average of the current and expectations components. The Conference Board consumer confidence index is defined as two-fifths of the present situation index plus three-fifths of the expectations index; hence, it is slightly more weighted to the six-month ahead expectations. The University of Michigan compiles their composite index based on five questions with a decidedly longer run horizon than that of the Conference Board's measure. The five University of Michigan questions are:

1. We are interested in how people are getting along financially these days. Would you say that you (and your family living there) are better off or worse off financially than you were a year ago?
2. Now looking ahead—do you think that a year from now

you (and your family living there) will be better off financially, or worse off, or just about the same as now?

3. Now turning to business conditions in the country as a whole—do you think that during the next 12 months we'll have good times financially, or bad times, or what?

4. Looking ahead, which would you say is more likely— that in the country as a whole we'll have continuous good times during the next five years or so, or that we will have periods of widespread unemployment or depression, or what?

5. About the big things people buy for their homes—such as furniture, a refrigerator, stove, television, and things like that. Generally speaking, do you think now is a good or bad time for people to buy major household items?

Sometimes the current and future expectations can move in opposite directions, which may be a key theme in understanding the report. For example, if tax increases are being discussed by Congress, then it is possible for the current conditions reading to be upbeat while the expectations component could be weak. Moreover, expectation indexes between the Conference Board and University of Michigan series could diverge because of the differences in their forecast horizons.

Although all three measures basically tell the same story over time, in the short term they can differ. On a monthly average basis—using the end of month observation, the ABC News poll was the least volatile between the onset of the 1990 recession and mid-1992, while the Michigan survey—which has the smallest sample size—was the most volatile. The University of Michigan's early month consumer confidence reading can have market impact—if it shows a sharp and unexpected rise or fall. The Conference Board measure often (though not always) will have a similar theme as the early University of Michigan poll, which makes the Conference Board release less of a surprise for the financial markets. The ABC News poll has a following but little or no financial market impact.

The statistical relationship between the University of Michigan consumer sentiment index and the Conference Board consumer confidence index suggests that every *one-point* change in the University of Michigan series will result in a *two-point* change in the Conference Board measure. Of course, the relationship between these measures, by construction, is not linear, so this result should be viewed only as a rough rule of thumb. Interestingly, the statistical combination of any two of the consumer surveys generally explained the third better than the individual surveys alone, which suggests that each contributes a slightly different and unique perspective on the consumer.

Consumer Conference over the Business Cycle

As would be expected, consumer confidence is the weakest during recessions, slightly better on average during recoveries, and the highest during expansions. Confidence is classified by the Commerce Department as a leading economic indicator

FIGURE 5–1a Conference Board's Consumer Confidence Index

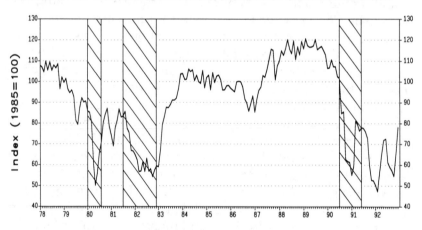

Note: Shaded areas represent business cycle recessions

FIGURE 5–1b Consumer Confidence Index, Conference Board
January 1978–December 1992, Index, 1985=100

| Period | Historic Low | Normal Bounds | | | Historic High | Series Characteristics | |
		Normal Low	Average	Normal High		Standard Deviation	Share of Total Observations
Recession	50.1% in May 1980	60.3%	65.7%	71.2%	85.7% in Aug 1981	10.9 pp.	30	16.7%
Recovery	47.3% in Feb 1992	69.1%	76.9%	84.8%	106.1% in Apr 1984	15.7 pp.	42	23.3%
Expansion	54.6% in Oct 1992	95.2%	101.5%	107.8%	120.7% in Feb 1989	12.6 pp.	108	60.0%

FIGURE 5–2a University of Michigan's Consumer Survey

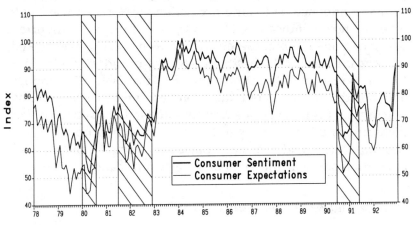

Note: Shaded areas represent business cycle recessions

FIGURE 5–2b Consumer Sentiment Index, University of Michigan

January 1978–December 1992, Index

		Normal Bounds				Series Characteristics	
Period	Historic Low	Normal Low	Average	Normal High	Historic High	Standard Deviation	Share of Total Observations
Recession	51.7% in May 1980	63.4 %	67.0%	70.6 %	87.7% in Mar 1991	7.2 pp.	30	16.7%
Recovery	64.5% in Dec 1980	75.5 %	80.6%	85.8 %	101.0% in Mar 1984	10.3 pp.	42	23.3%
Expansion	60.4% in Jul 1979	82.2 %	87.3%	92.5 %	100.9% in Sep 1984	10.3 pp.	108	60.0%

based on its timing relationship with the business cycle. (See Figures 5–1a, 5–1b, 5–2a, 5–2b.)

Special Factors, Limitations, and Other Data Issues

In the late 1950s and again after the 1987 stock market crash, consumer confidence surveys have come under attack by economists. Economists questioned how useful consumer confidence surveys were for predicting consumer spending. Some of the critics suggested that consumer confidence told us nothing about future consumer spending. But most of the literature—especially, the more recent studies—seemed to conclude that consumer confidence had some predictive value when used with other economic indicators. However, one of the most important uses for consumer confidence has been totally overlooked; namely, it is one of the best predictors of presidential elections. In many respects, this should not be surprising. Perceptions, and not the reality, about the economy influence presidential outcomes. This point seems well founded in the political science literature, and it might suggest that a president who is a "great communicator" and can shape perceptions could enhance one's re-election or the incumbent party's election chances.

Relationship with Other Series

The University of Michigan's consumer expectations subcomponent index is used in the monthly calculation of the BEA's composite index of leading economic indicators. But by the time the leading economic indicator composite is released, a new reading of the current month's consumer expectations index is available.

Despite all the concern that consumer confidence is a driving force behind consumer spending, confidence is not a particularly reliable precursor of consumer spending. Often, consumer confidence and consumer spending will rise and fall at the same time, and sometimes spending increases will precede a pickup in confidence. Moreover, some marketing research even has shown that when consumers are depressed, that has triggered spending. So the relationship between spending and confidence may be more fancy than fact.

References

Friend, Irwin and F. Gerald Adams, "The Predictive Ability of Consumer Attitudes, Stock Prices, and Non-Attitudinal Variables," *Journal of the American Statistical Association*, Vol. 59 (No. 308), December 1964, pp. 987–1005.

Fuhrer, Jeffrey C., "On the Information Content of Consumer Survey Expectations," *The Review of Economics and Statistics*, 1988, pp. 140–144.

Garner, C. Alan, "Forecasting Consumer Spending: Should Economists

Pay Attention to Consumer Confidence Surveys?" *Economic Review,* Federal Reserve Bank of Kansas City, May/June 1991, pp. 57–71.

Niemira, Michael P., "What's the Relationship Among Consumer Confidence Surveys?" *Business Economics,* April 1992, pp. 65–66.

Chapter 6

Consumer Credit

General Description

The Federal Reserve Board's consumer credit release details the amount of installment credit that individuals (consumers) have outstanding. It is defined as a loan that is scheduled to be repaid in two or more installments. It does not include mortgage debt or any other loan secured by real estate.

Economic Indicator Information at a Glance

Market Significance	Low
Typical Release Time	2:00 PM Eastern Time Fifth Business Day of the Month
Released By	Federal Reserve
Month Covered	Two Months Prior

The consumer credit data is broken down into three types of credit and by the type of institution holding the debt. The three credit categories are automobile credit, revolving credit, and all other. Included in the last category (but not restricted to) are mobile home loans, education loans, and vacation loans. The proportions of each type of debt at the end of 1992 were automobile (35 percent), revolving (34 percent), and other (31 percent). The types of holders range from commercial banks to retailers to gasoline companies and pools of securitized assets. In the 1980s, there was tremendous growth in the packaging of credit card debt and automobile debt and selling the sum total as a single collateralized security. When this was done, the debt was taken off the institution's books, creating the need to account for this still existing debt, a hole filled by the latter category. (See Figure 6–1.)

FIGURE 6–1 Major Holders of Consumer Installment Debt: End of 1992 Percentage

Commercial Banks	46%
Finance Companies	17%
Credit Unions	13%
Securitized Assets	13%
Saving Institutions	5.6%
Retailers	5.4%
Gasoline Companies	0.6%

Figures may not add to one hundred due to rounding.

Analyzing the Data

What analysis is undertaken is very simple. The market looks at the size of the change in consumer credit. Even spurious monthly component changes, which can be fairly frequent, or strong evidence that the credit data defy existing sales data in a specific area (i.e., automobiles), are typically ignored by the market. Beyond the immediate market response, it is difficult justifying much time spent analyzing the information provided.

By the time the consumer credit number is released, the market has already seen actual spending data. Retail sales figures and even more complete personal consumption expenditure data for the same month come out two to three weeks prior to the consumer credit statistics. Thus, the data just provide us with an idea (however inaccurate) of how much of already known spending was financed. In this respect, it is of little market significance. As much as consumer attitudes towards the use of credit to finance purchases may have some conceptual importance, there is no evidence that this percentage changes before actual spending habits change. Thus, an upturn in spending growth typically will be accompanied by a consequent or subsequent upturn in consumer credit. The consumer credit data merely validates spending trends; it doesn't reveal new ones. Futhermore, there are some technical reasons why consumer credit is of suspicious value.

Two developing trends in the 1980s have caused consumer installment debt to miss key elements of consumer spending power. One is the growing move towards leasing automobiles. The credit series misses these "purchases," which grew to 23 percent of the consumer car market in 1992. This is part of the reason that the auto component of consumer credit has had such a poor relationship with actual sales. Between February 1990 and December 1991, consumer automobile-installment credit fell every month; 22 months to be exact. Over the same period, monthly unit sales of automobiles fell only 11 times. The largest monthly drop in the automobile component over that period was $3.6 bn. in May 1991, a month in which unit auto sales actually rose 4.4 percent.

The second problem with the consumer installment credit data is its exclusion of credit secured by real estate—the key issue being home equity loans. Tax law changes in the 1980s, which denied tax deductions for nonreal estate interest payments, have pushed consumers to pay down revolving credit outstanding and to "refinance" it with home equity loans, the interest on which is tax deductible. Similarly, home equity loans have become an effective way to finance an automobile purchase. With these credit extensions absent from the consumer credit series, a misleading picture is presented of consumers' financial position and their willingness to take on debt.

It is somewhat difficult to detail a typical market response to consumer credit. Superficially, strong (weak) credit growth would be negative (positive) for fixed-income instruments and positive (negative) for equities and the dollar. But all is not as it seems. One could also say that the greater the credit growth, the closer the consumer is to being overextended, with the next step being a slowing of consumption and economic activity. Under that interpretation, a spurt in consumer credit would be positive for the fixed-income markets and negative for equities and the greenback. Although the initial interpretive reaction is typical,

FIGURE 6–2a Consumer Credit Outstanding

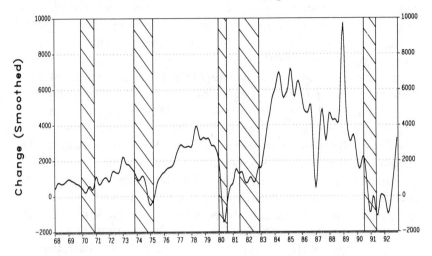

Note: Shaded areas represent business cycle recessions

FIGURE 6–2b Consumer Credit Outstanding
(January 1948–December 1992, Change, Billions of Dollars

Period	Historic Low	Normal Bounds			Historic High	Series Characteristics	
		Normal Low	Average	Normal High		Standard Deviation	Share of Total Observations
Recession	−$3.3 bn. in Dec 1990	−$0.2 bn	$0.3 bn.	$0.8 bn	+$3.6 bn. in Sep 1981	$1.0 bn.	96	18.1%
Recovery	−$2.7 bn. in Apr 1992	$0.2 bn	$1.1 bn.	$2.0 bn	+$7.5 bn. in Mar 1984	$1.8 bn.	123	23.3%
Expansion	−$1.5 bn. in Jan 1987	$0.6 bn	$1.8 bn.	$3.1 bn	+$25.0 bn. in Jan 1989	$2.4 bn.	310	58.6%

one can never be sure when the market will choose the latter. It is just one more reason to take the consumer credit data lightly.

Consumer Credit over the Business Cycle

Net consumer credit outstanding shows a pronounced and expected business cycle pattern. During recessions net credit outstanding behaves similarly to nominal consumer spending; that is, it increases, on average, but at a much reduced pace. A recovery sees a marked improvement in the average increase in net consumer credit outstanding, although the expansion phase still accounts for the largest average gains in net consumer credit outstanding. (See Figures 6–2a, 6–2b.)

Chapter 7

Consumer Price Index

General Description

The Consumer Price Index (CPI) measures the average change in prices of a fixed basket of goods and services. There are two measures of the rate of inflation at the consumer level. The first is the CPI-U, and it is the focal point of financial markets. It measures price changes for all urban consumers, which encompasses approximately 80 percent of the population. The second price measure is the CPI-W. It measures price changes for all urban wage earners and covers about 50 percent of the population.

Economic Indicator Information at a Glance

Market Significance	High
Typical Release Time	8:30 AM Eastern Time Around the Tenth Business Day of the Month
Released By	Labor Department Bureau of Labor Statistics
Month Covered	Prior Month

The reason for two similar price measures is grounded in politics, not economics. In the late 1970s (the CPI-W was officially introduced in January 1978) when inflation was rampant, labor leaders were convinced that inflation faced by workers was greater than that portrayed by the CPI-U. As a concession to labor, the CPI-W was created, and cost of living increases in union contracts were generated from it. At best, there is only a marginal difference between the inflation rates of the two series since only the component weightings differ.

Prices are collected in 91 urban areas around the country with more than 19,000 retail establishments and 57,000 housing units included (the housing units are for pricing housing costs). All taxes included in the final purchase price are part of the calculation. Price changes for items covered in the CPI are calculated for each area and then averaged together to form a national average.

Although the Bureau of Labor Statistics (BLS) publishes a seasonally adjusted rate of change, it does not publish a seasonally adjusted index for the total CPI. Furthermore, there are no revisions to prior months' data with each CPI release. All revisions are incorporated in the annual revisions released each February, and even then only components are subject to change. The an-

---

Housing Costs and the CPI

In the late 1970s and early 1980s, mortgage rates and home prices were skyrocketing. This had a very strong effect on the CPI, since both were among the factors upon which the Bureau of Labor Statistics calculated home ownership costs. It was a realistic method, and there was no issue about the veracity of the rise in these costs. But this was a time when rising, double-digit inflation was a very sensitive political issue. Much was made of the fact that not everyone bought a house; most families rent. Therefore, the CPI was overstating the rate of inflation faced by the majority of consumers.

As a result of this criticism, in January 1983, the BLS formally switched to what is called "owner's equivalent rent." This measure of housing costs excludes actual interest costs and housing prices and determines home ownership costs by estimating what it would cost owners to rent their house. Interestingly, this method has come under criticism in the early 1990s. Now, it is said to overstate inflation . . . because it does not pick up the weakness in housing prices or declining mortgage rates!

nual rate of change is not revised. The reason for this is the numerous cost-of-living clauses in labor contracts or government programs tied to the CPI. If there were to be revisions to prior years, it could create havoc regarding past payments.

The most basic division of the CPI is between goods and services. The former accounts for 44.1 percent of the index and services for 55.9 percent. There are some general rules concerning the inflation trends of the two sectors. One is that the goods sector inflation is more volatile than service sector inflation. The chief reason is that the goods or commodity sector is heavily influenced by food and energy prices. These two areas account for approximately one-half of the commodity component. Energy services, however, account for only about 6 percent of service sector prices. As will be discussed, price changes in these two areas are especially volatile. A second rule is that service sector inflation is less volatile over the business cycle. Its movement from troughs to peaks is much less extreme than commodity sector inflation. A third rule, somewhat linked to the second, is that service sector inflation lags commodity inflation. Its peaks and troughs (on average) are about six to nine months behind those in the goods sector.

Another decomposition—and the one the markets focus on the most—is the breakdown of the CPI into the food, energy, and all other areas. The latter is referred to (somewhat obviously) as the CPI ex food and energy, or more colloquially as the "core" rate of inflation. The purpose of "ex-ing" out the food and energy components is that these two components often are much more volatile than the core rate. This being the case, they can give a false impression of underlying demand-driven inflationary pressures. (See Figure 7–1.)

FIGURE 7–1 CPI: Annual Inflation Rates: 1984–1992
Food, Energy and Core
December-over-December Percentage Change

Year	1984	1985	1986	1987	1988	1989	1990	1991	1992
Core rate	4.7%	4.3%	3.8%	4.2%	4.7%	4.4%	5.2%	4.2%	3.3%
Energy	0.2	1.8	-19.7	8.2	0.5	5.1	18.1	-7.4	2.0
Food	3.8	2.6	3.8	3.5	5.2	5.6	5.3	1.9	1.5

Source: Bureau of Labor Statistics

One final categorization is by major purchase groups. (See Figure 7–2.) There can be specific lower levels of detail that are of interest to the markets, such as car prices and tobacco prices, because they can have an unusually strong effect on a given monthly CPI. However, in general the major purchase groups are the lowest level at which market relevant analysis is conducted.

Analyzing the Data

The immediate focus of the markets when the CPI is released is the month-to-month change for the overall CPI and for the core rate, with the core rate usually carrying more weight than the overall inflation reading. Less interest is paid to the translation of the month-to-month change to an annual rate or to the year-to-year inflation rate for a given month. Readings that are two-tenths or more from expectations (above or below, of

FIGURE 7–2 CPI: Relative Importance of Major Components: December 1992*

By Key Market Grouping	
Ex Food and Energy	76.93
Food and Beverage	17.40
Energy	7.29
By Major Purchase Category**	
Food and Beverage	17.40
Housing	41.40
Apparel and Upkeep	6.00
Transportation	17.01
Medical Care	6.90
Entertainment	4.35
Other Goods and Services	6.90

*Because these are relative importance measures, not weights, they do not necessarily add to 100.

**In this breakdown, energy prices do not have separate billing. They are distributed throughout other sectors, showing up among other places in the housing component and the transportation component.

FIGURE 7–3a Consumer Price Index

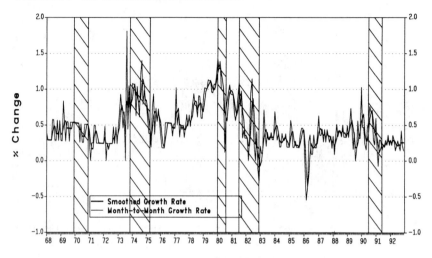

Note: Shaded areas represent business cycle recessions

FIGURE 7–3b Consumer Price Index
January 1948–December 1992, Percent Change

Period	Historic Low	Normal Bounds			Historic High	Series Characteristics		
		Normal Low	Average	Normal High		Standard Deviation	Share of Total Observations	
Recession	−0.8% in Jul 1949	0.2 %	0.4 %	0.6 %	+1.4% in Sep 1974	0.4 pp.	96	18.1%
Recovery	−0.4% in Jan 1950	0.2 %	0.3 %	0.5 %	+1.1% in Nov 1980	0.3 pp.	123	23.3%
Expansion	−0.5% in Mar 1986	0.2 %	0.3 %	0.5 %	+1.8% in Aug 1973	0.3 pp.	310	58.6%

course) are large enough to significantly affect the markets and potentially hold a new inflation story.

Once the market has absorbed the inflation readings in the core, energy and food sectors, attention is turned quickly to the source of any surprises in the core area. The typical breakdown is into the six previously mentioned categories, such as housing, transportation, and so forth. The greater the number of areas that contributed to any surprising change, the higher the likelihood the result will sharply affect the subsequent behavior of financial markets.

FIGURE 7–4a Consumer Price Index Less Food and Energy

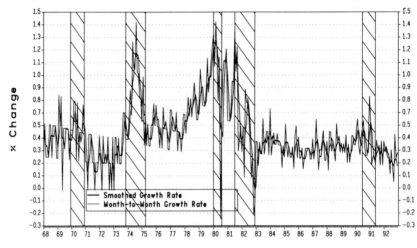

Note: Shaded areas represent business cycle recessions

FIGURE 7–4b Consumer Price Index Less Food and Energy
February 1957–December 1992, Percent Change

		Normal Bounds				Series Characteristics	
Period	Historic Low	Normal Low	Average	Normal High	Historic High	Standard Deviation	Share of Total Observations
Recession	−0.3% in Jul 1960	0.3 %	0.5 %	0.7 %	+1.4% in Mar 1980	0.4 pp.	96	18.1%
Recovery	−0.1% in Dec 1982	0.3 %	0.4 %	0.5 %	+1.2% in Dec 1980	0.2 pp.	123	23.3%
Expansion	−0.3% in Jan 1963	0.3 %	0.4 %	0.6 %	+1.4% in Jul 1981	0.3 pp.	310	58.6%

It is difficult finding a consistent level of dissection beyond these six categories. Most times they will serve the very useful and necessary function of determining the breadth of any price change. However, analysts and the markets also develop a sense of which sectors, over particular spans of time, are most likely to be the source of intermittent price shocks. Car prices are a sector that has consistently been a culprit in monthly inflationary surprises. Tobacco prices, a sector that might take the title as having the economy's lowest price sensitivity, have been a major source of monthly inflation discrepancies also. When the surprises come in sectors known to be unusually volatile, the markets are more likely to dismiss any aberrant inflation reading even more than if the price pressures stemmed from two sectors unfamiliar to the market.

More so for inflation data than for just about any other economic data, financial markets (especially the bond market) that are particularly willing to assume surprises are just onetime occurrences. Thus, a strong CPI reading that is fueled by a burst in energy prices will be dismissed in an environment in which there is no reason to believe that oil prices are poised for a sustained rise. Of course, the opposite works as well; a weak energy price reading in the midst of a bullish oil market would be glossed over. But even if there is breadth to a particular month's surprise, if it contrasts with the market's fundamental views of underlying inflationary pressures (i.e., a strong reading in a low inflationary environment or a weak reading in a high inflationary environment), there often is not a lasting trading response to a surprising CPI.

Consumer Prices over the Business Cycle

The first thing to note is that inflation has its own cycle, one that lags the growth cycle (see Appendix II). For this reason, looking at average month-to-month changes for the CPI can be misleading, as they are pretty much identical during each phase of the business cycle. This pertains to the core CPI rate as well. In fact, the core rate shows a more stable pattern throughout the cycle than does the overall CPI. Historic highs and lows for the core CPI are matched in the recession and expansion phases and only two-tenths different than during the recovery. (See Figures 7–3a, 7–3b, 7–4a, 7–4b.)

Chapter 8

Durable Goods Orders and Shipments

General Description

The report on durable goods orders is one part of a series of manufacturing and trade reports that continually gets "built into" other more comprehensive reports on the manufacturing and trade sector. The market focus of this report is new orders, though the report contains data on shipments and unfilled orders. Because these new orders data can be quite volatile, the market often can be surprised by the strength or weakness in the orders' data, but the financial market reaction is often limited for the same reason.

Economic Indicator Information at a Glance

Market Significance	Moderate
Typical Release Time	8:30 AM Eastern Time About 18th Business Day
Released By	Commerce Department Census Bureau
Period Covered	Prior Month

The underlying survey used to collect shipments, new and unfilled orders, and inventories for durable goods, as well as the more encompassing manufacturing report, is completed by companies on a voluntary basis. The survey information is collected in several alternative ways, including the traditional "form," by telephone (both voice and computer assisted), and by facsimile. It includes most manufacturing firms with 1,000 employees or more and representative smaller ones. Generally, companies with less than 100 employees are not sampled but estimated from industry averages.

New orders are defined as the intent to buy for immediate or future delivery. A new order must be supported by binding legal documents (i.e., signed purchase agreements, letters of intent or award, etc.). The monthly series for new orders measures the current month's orders less cancellations.

To insure consistency within the shipments and orders' data collected by the Census Bureau, *new orders are derived* from backlogs and shipments data using the identity:

New Orders= Change in Unfilled Orders + Shipments

Several components of the new orders detail are equal to shipments, by definition, since those industries do not maintain backlogs. The most notable category where this occurs is with motor vehicles. Motor vehicle orders are assumed in this report to be the same as the value of car and truck assemblies. Hence, watching auto and truck production schedules is one way to anticipate the possible strength or weakness in durable goods orders. But besides that category, this "new orders equals shipments" assumption is also true for lumber, farm machinery, metal cans, glass containers, and other transportation equipment.

Analyzing the Data

Certain "high-value" sectors can dominate the change in these data, so it is appropriate to view durable goods orders excluding some extremely volatile sectors such as defense and transportation. Defense orders accounted for about 5 to 6 percent of total orders in 1992 but contributed about 50 percent of the variability. Similarly, transportation orders, which accounted for about 25 percent of total orders and can be dominated by swings in high-value aircraft orders, often add to the choppiness of the overall orders series. Hence, *total durable goods orders less defense orders* and *total orders less transportation orders* are two key measures to watch to understand the underlying trend. However, it is not possible to isolate defense orders from transportation orders, which means that a sharp upward or downward move in the defense component can still have a pronounced effect on the major industry detail, such as transportation, primary metals, and so forth. As such, *impressions* of the strength or weakness of this report can still be dominated by a narrowly based increase in defense or transportation. Another important component to watch is nondefense capital goods orders, especially without aircraft and parts. Nondefense capital goods orders less aircraft and parts account for about one-fifth of the total and often can be a better guide to the underlying strength or weakness in orders since it excludes most (but by no means all) of the extremely volatile components. It includes: (1) nondefense portions of ordnance, (2) steam, gas, and hydraulic turbines, (3) internal combustion engines, (4) construction, mining, and material handling equipment, (5) metalworking machinery, (6) special industry machinery, (7) electrical transmission and distribution equipment, (8) electrical industrial apparatus, (9) communications equipment, (10) railroad equipment, and (11) search and navigation equipment. Finally, another useful measure is consumer goods. Consumer goods and materials orders are not actually shown in the report, but by definition the total less capital goods leaves consumer goods and materials. However, that component can be dominated at times by swings in car production. (See Figure 8–1.)

FIGURE 8–1 The Major Component Shares of New Orders for Durable Goods

	1992 Shares
Total Durable Goods	100.0%
Consumer Goods and Materials	69.5
Capital goods	30.5
Nondefense Capital Goods	24.9
Nondefense Captial Goods Less Aircraft and Parts	20.9
Defense Captial Goods	5.6

Durable Goods Orders over the Business Cycle

Durable goods new orders have a typical-cycle pattern with the strongest gains in the recovery phase of the cycle. On average, durable orders increase by 1.5 percent per month during the recovery and then moderate to about half that pace during the expansion. There is a good deal of variability in these data, as reflected by the large standard deviation around the mean of about four percentage points. (See Figures 8–2a and 8–3b.) Unfilled orders, on the other hand, tend to expand the most during the expansion phase (as expected) when demand exceeds supply. Unfilled orders should not be the focus of the market's attention until capacity utilization notches up over 83 percent, since backlogs will be drawn down even in a recovery due to the slack in capacity utilization. (See Figures 8–3a and 8–3b.)

FIGURE 8–2a Durable Goods New Orders

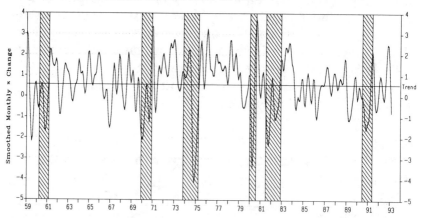

Note: Shaded areas represent business cycle recessions

FIGURE 8–2b Durable Goods New Orders
(1960–1992, Percent Change)

		Normal Bounds				Series Characteristics	
Period	Historic Low	Normal Low	Average	Normal High	Historic High	Standard Deviation	Share of Total Observations
Recession	−10.7% in Nov 1990	−3.0%	−1.0%	+1.0%	+8.3% in Jul 1980	4.0 pp.	67	17.0%
Recovery	−7.5% in Apr 1984	−0.3%	+1.5%	+3.3%	+12.1% in Jul 1991	3.6 pp.	92	23.4%
Expansion	−8.3% in Jan 1990	−0.9%	+0.7%	+2.3%	+11.1% in Jan 1964	3.2 pp.	235	59.6%

FIGURE 8–3a Durable Goods Unfilled Orders

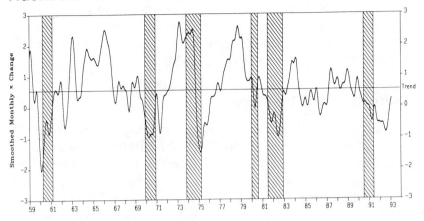

Note: Shaded areas represent business cycle recessions

FIGURE 8–3b Durable Goods Unfilled Orders
(1960–1992, Percent Change)

| Period | Historic Low | Normal Bounds | | | Historic High | Series Characteristics | |
		Normal Low	Average	Normal High		Standard Deviation	Share of Total Observations
Recession	−1.8% in Oct 1960	−0.7%	−0.1%	+0.5%	+3.3% in Aug 1974	1.2 pp.	67	17.0%
Recovery	−1.5% in Jun 1975	−0.3%	+0.2%	+0.7%	+2.8% in Mar 1984	1.0 pp.	92	23.4%
Expansion	−2.3% in Feb 1960	+0.4%	+0.9%	+1.4%	+3.4% in Mar 1973	1.0 pp.	235	59.6%

Special Factors, Limitations, and Other Data Issues

Despite the importance of unfilled orders in the derivation of new orders, measuring unfilled orders is extremely difficult because this statistic is often not required for financial and tax reporting purposes of a company. Moreover, the Commerce Department has found that there are often differences in how that statistic is measured among those firms that actually produce such a measure. Hence, the Commerce Department allows firms to report unfilled orders as observed (if they exist), or they can be calculated by the reporting company using the previous definition. The bottom line is that little should be read into a single month's report, but the longer term trends (e.g., three-month horizon) often provide a better reading.

One additional background point in interpreting these orders and shipments data is to remember that they are not adjusted for inflation. Hence, a comparison of today's new orders growth with the pace during the 1970s is biased by the higher inflation of the 1970s compared to the early 1990s.

Relationship with Other Series

Machine tool orders data, which are compiled by the trade association—the National Machine Tool Builders Association—generally are reported on the last Monday of every month and may be reported before the durable goods report. Although machine tool orders are conceptually covered in the durable goods report, they represent less than 0.5 percent of total durable goods orders. Moreover, on a year-over-year basis, machine tool orders are more than five times as volatile as durable goods orders, which makes looking at machine tool orders relatively useless as a forecaster of the Commerce series. Still, over long periods the series profile is broadly similar.

Announced aircraft orders by the major producers such as Boeing and McDonnell Douglas are often looked at as a harbinger of the comparable component of the durable goods orders report. However, as little as 10 percent of the announced orders actually are booked in that given month, which clearly cautions against reading too much into the announcements. In some cases, airlines have requested that their aircraft order announcement be delayed for internal company reasons. In other cases, federal government approval is required prior to a sale being consummated. Finally, aircraft cancellations can also depress any given month's aircraft orders.

The durable goods report is important for the computation of the composite index of leading economic indicators, which draws three of the total 11 components from this report—new orders for nondefense capital goods, new orders for consumer goods, and unfilled orders. Hence, economists will often revise their leading indicator forecast after the release of the durable goods report.

Finally, the nondefense durable goods shipments less aircraft and parts component of this report is one "source" or input series used for deriving the producers' durable goods measure of the GDP report.

Chapter 9

Employment Report

General Description

Employment is the single most important economic series for the financial markets because it is very timely and quite comprehensive. As such, this report is often a focus of politicians and monetary policy officials. Employment is viewed as one of the best concurrent measure of business activity, although studies have shown that employment as well as the unemployment rate typically are lagging economic indicators of output changes.

Economic Indicator Information at a Glance

Market Significance	Very High
Typical Release Time	8:30 AM Eastern Time First Friday of the Month
Released By	Department of Labor Bureau of Labor Statistics
Period Covered	Prior Month

Analyzing the Data

The Labor Department reports two independently derived measures of employment on a monthly basis. The *establishment* measure is based on payroll records, which measures employment in nonagricultural industries. The second measure, *household employment*, is based on a survey and measures civilian noninstitutional employment aged 16 years and older (14 years and older before 1967), which includes agricultural workers and the self-employed. The household series is derived the Current Population Survey (CPS), which is a monthly rotating sample of about 60,000 households. About three-fourths of the sample is the same for any two months. The unemployment rate is computed based on the household survey measures of employment and labor force. The payroll series measures the *number of jobs* (which includes double-counting from multiple jobholders) while the household measure counts the number of people that are working. Over the long run, the household and payroll measures of employment have similar fluctuation and can be used as a cross-check on each other. However, for any given month it is possible to have the two measures move in opposite directions.

The monthly employment release spans many more concepts that fill in the employment picture by age, race, sex, type of occupation, and by state. Some of the other commonly used terminology from the employment report is described on the following page.

Some keys to interpret the employment report should include:

- View the monthly change in employment—household and payroll—in a business cycle context and use the two series as a cross-check on each other for the month. Look at the manufacturing payroll employment change as a sensitive cyclical measure of business conditions.
- Do not lose sight of longer term themes such as the contraction in the defense-related industries, restructuring in an industry, and so forth. These themes are likely to drive the future trend of employment.
- Be aware of any additional strike activity that may have occurred during the month that could weaken a given month's employment change or the return of strikers, which could boost payroll employment.
- Recognize that the unemployment rate (inverted) is a leading indicator at business cycle peaks but a lagging indicator at business cycle troughs.
- Watch the length of the workweek, since businesses adjust hours before employment and those short-term adjust-

Workforce Terms

Unemployment Rate: The unemployment rate is defined as the difference between the labor force (LF) and the employed workforce (E) divided by the labor force times 100; that is, rate = 100 × (LF–E)/LF. The BLS also calculates alternative measures of the unemployment rate, designated as U-1 to U-7, which are more or less inclusive. The standard civilian unemployment rate is also designated as U-5b.

Labor Force Participation Rate: This measure is the share of the civilian noninstitutional population that is 16 years and over that is in the labor force.

Discouraged Workers: The BLS household asks individuals answering the survey whether they want a job and if they answer "yes," they then are asked if they are looking for a job. If they answer "no" because they "believe no work is available," they are classified as a discouraged worker and not counted as part of the labor force.

Employment Diffusion Index: This index measures the percentage of industries in which employment was growing. The index is defined as the percentage of the group of industries (total or manufacturing) that showed an increase over the stated period (one-, three-, six-, or twelve-month spans) plus one-half of the percentage of those industries that showed no change. Hence, a reading of 50 percent means no change. Above 50 percent implies more industries increased employment than cut back and vice-versa for an index reading of less than 50 percent. Julius Shiskin, a former Commissioner of the BLS, once suggested the employment diffusion index was a key measure to determine whether the economy was in a recession.

ES-202 Report: The payroll employment data is "benchmarked" (i.e., an annual adjustment to more comprehensive counts of employment) from the so-called ES-202 program. The E2-202 program is named after the form that employers file with their state unemployment insurance offices. On that form, the company reports the number of employees. About 50 percent of all companies have less than 500 employees—the typical Small Business Administration definition of a small business. Unfortunately, since 1984 reporting changes have tended to inflate the small business category. Since 1984 an effort has been made to break out multi-establishments. That means that a large employer reporting before 1984 could be a small business (by definition) in subsequent years solely due to the employer reporting each store, plant, or facility separately instead of as a single company total.

ES-790 Report: This is the monthly payroll report title that is filed by firms with the states showing their employment. These reports are then consolidated by the states and reported back to BLS.

Okun's Law: The late Arthur Okun—a former member of the Council of Economic Advisers—formulated a rule of thumb between real growth and its impact on the unemployment rate. Although Okun later rescinded what has become known as "Okun's Law," most economists still use the concept. It provides a ballpark estimate of the real GDP growth needed to budge the unemployment rate. Our recent update of that rule, using a variant suggested by the Federal Reserve Bank of Atlanta some years ago, implies that real GDP growth of 2.3 percent is the threshold that needs to be exceeded for an impact on the unemployment rate. Indeed, the rule suggests that each 1 percentage point higher growth trims the unemployment rate by 0.07 percentage points in the current quarter. If real GDP growth averages 3 percent per quarter during a given year, then this rule of thumb suggests that the unemployment rate will be trimmed by about 0.2 percentage points by year end.

---

ments more readily reflect private sector demand changes.

- Be careful not to overinterpret month-over-month changes in average hourly earnings (a wage measure); it is volatile and conceptually flawed because it does not hold employment shares constant. Year-over-year growth in average hourly earnings provides a better, though still incomplete, picture of wage trends.

Characteristics of the Household Data

The employment data are collected for a single week (Sunday through Saturday) of the month that includes the 12th day. An employed person for the survey is defined as: (1) all civilians who during the survey week were paid for any work performed by them or were self-employed (a business, professional practice, or farm) and (2) all persons who did not work temporarily due to illness, bad weather, vacation, labor-management disputes, or personal reasons—whether paid or unpaid, but had jobs or a business. Unemployed persons are those that made efforts to find work within the preceding four-week period, or were waiting to be recalled to a job from which they were laid off, or were waiting to report to a job within the next 30 days. These unemployment data are classified by duration and reason for unemployment. From these data, it is possible to tell how long the unemployed have been out of a job and whether the job loss was temporary or permanent. On the employment side, the length of the individual's workweek is collected, which allows the BLS to report statistics on full- and part-time employment. The sum of the unemployed and the employed is the labor force.

Household Employment Behavior over the Business Cycle

The household data is used for the calculation of the unemployment rate. Typically, labor force growth picks up once the economy is beginning to show signs of improvement. Discouraged workers (i.e., those individuals who dropped out of the labor force since they felt it was futile to look for a job) tend to return to the labor force, and labor force growth tends to outpace household employment growth. This puts upward pressure on the unemployment rate and conceptually accounts for its classification as a lagging cyclical indicator by the Commerce Department. This point is exemplified over the 1980–1992 period when the unemployment rate averaged 7.9 percent during recessions, 8.1 percent during recoveries, and 6.4 percent during expansions. In a relative sense, household employment tends to grow faster during recoveries than during expansions. The average increase during recoveries was 185K persons, compared to a 150K-person average increase during expansions. In the early stages of the recovery, household employment growth tends to be stronger than payroll employment growth mainly due to self-employment growth. Self-employment tends to grow faster in the recovery compared to company hirings.

The broader coverage of the household employment compared to the payroll measure, which in 1992 amounted to about 10 million people (and maybe more if the double-counting in the payroll report could be eliminated), provides some unique insights on the labor markets that cannot be discerned from looking solely at the payroll data. (See Figure 9–1.)

Characteristics of the Payroll Data

The payroll employment statistic is collected for the week that includes the 12th. These data tend to be less volatile than

FIGURE 9–1 Industry Shares of Payroll Employment

	1992	1991	1990	1989	1988
Total Payroll	100.0%	100.0%	100.0%	100.0%	100.0%
Goods Producing	21.6	22.0	22.7	23.4	23.9
Mining	0.6	0.6	0.6	0.6	0.7
Construction	4.2	4.3	4.7	4.8	4.8
Manufacturing	16.8	17.0	17.4	17.9	18.3
Motor Vehicle Equipment	0.7	0.7	0.7	0.8	0.8
Defense-Related	1.1	1.2	1.3	1.3	1.4
Other Mfg.	15.0	15.1	15.4	15.8	16.1
Service Producing	78.4	78.0	77.3	76.6	76.1
Private Services	61.3	61.0	60.6	60.2	59.7
Retail	17.6	17.8	17.9	18.0	18.1
Services	26.7	26.1	25.6	25.0	24.3
Other Private	17.0	17.1	17.1	17.2	17.3
Government	17.1	17.0	16.7	16.4	16.5
Federal	2.7	2.7	2.8	2.8	2.8
State and Local	14.4	14.3	13.9	13.6	13.7
Employment by Establishment Size (Shares)*					
	1992	1991	1990		
Small-Business Dominated	—	44.8%	44.7%		

*As measured by the Small Business Administration (SBA) for December of year using BLS employment data. Some industries cannot be classified into small or large business based on the SBA definition that the industry is 60 percent or more dominated by a given size of firm.

the household series. A bias adjustment factor is included in the estimate of payroll employment to capture hiring by new businesses that are not yet accounted for by the BLS's sample. The bias factor, which has been the source of much controversy, is determined by a statistical time series model that conceptually should increase as new business incorporations occur. Payroll employment covers about 500 industries and is based on a sample of 340,000 firms. Hours worked and earnings also are collected from these same firms. Aggregate hours is the combination of the hours worked with the level of employment, which is the most comprehensive measure of business activity in the monthly report. However, hours worked and the aggregate hours series are measured only for the private sector. From a cyclical standpoint, hours tend to increase before employment does. In the late 1980s and early 1990s, employers had pushed the workweek to record lengths in an effort to hold employment levels and costs, which has lengthened the lead time between hours and new hiring.

Payroll employment is not strictly available by establishment size; however, the U.S. Small Business Administration (SBA) has calculated a concept dubbed "small-business dominated" and "large-business dominated" employment to track the progress of small business using the monthly BLS data. However, SBA also analyzes more comprehensive employment data by firm size, as is shown in Figure 9–2. The SBA data provide some

FIGURE 9–2 Private Nonfarm Establishment Employment Shares by Size of Firms

Shares—1988–90

	1988	1989	1990	Cumulative Growth
Small Business	54.5%	53.9%	53.7%	4.7%
Less than 20 Employees	20.9	20.3	20.2	3.2
20–99 Employees	19.2	18.9	18.9	5.2
100–499 Employees	14.5	14.6	14.5	6.1
Large Business (More than 500 Employees)	45.5	46.1	46.3	8.4

Source: Small Business Administration (SBA) based on U.S. Census data. Note these data are not strictly consistent with prior data released by the SBA, which were based on Dun & Bradstreet files.

perspective on the often-heard view that small business must be the engine of future employment growth. However, these data do not support that claim. Indeed, the smallest firms within small business also saw the slowest employment growth between 1988 and 1990. Finally, there is an ongoing controversy between the calculation of the national payroll employment estimate and an estimate that is calculated (by analysts) from the sum-of-the-states employment estimates. The BLS, which does not officially release the sum-of-the-states measure, attributes those differences mainly to methodology differences.

Payroll Employment Behavior over the Business Cycle

Unlike the monthly changes in household employment, payroll employment tends to grow faster in expansions than during the recovery phase of the cycle—which reflects the lagging nature of employment compared to output measures. During a recovery, payroll employment increases at an average of 176K persons per month with a normal range of +79K to +274K. Although a 200K person range around the average may seem large, it is not really, because it represents about 0.1 percent around its average. But still, the financial markets often read far too much into the monthly fluctuation than is often warranted. Moreover, during recovery phases of the business cycle, the standard deviation—a measure of volatility—in payroll employment changes is greater on a monthly basis than either in the expansion or recession phases. There are two other factors that should be kept in mind in interpreting changes in payroll employment, which are: (1) revisions and (2) special factors, such as strikes and temporary hiring for elections, summer jobs, and so forth. (See Figures 9–3a, 9–3b, 9–4a, 9–4b, 9–5a, 9–5b.)

Special Factors, Limitations, and Other Data Issues

Payroll employment data are affected by strikes, weather disruptions, holidays, and temporary hiring, such as government hiring associated with decade Census, federal government-funded summer jobs programs, workers hired to work on election day at the polls, etc., and workers involved in military re-

FIGURE 9–3a Payroll Employment Changes

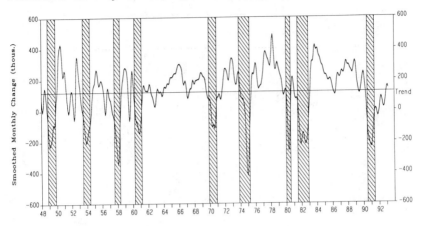

Note: Shaded areas represent business cycle recessions

FIGURE 9–3b Payroll Employment Changes
(January 1948–December 1992, Thousands of Jobs)

Period	Historic Low	Normal Bounds			Historic High	Series Characteristics		
		Normal Low	Average	Normal High		Standard Deviation	Share of Total Observations	
Recession	−885 K in Oct 1949	−248 K	−157 K	−66 K	+218 K in Sep 1949	182 K	96	18.1%
Recovery	−339 K in Aug 1983	+79 K	+176 K	+274 K	+1149 K in Sep 1983	195 K	123	23.3%
Expansion	−690 K in Jul 1956	+105 K	+184 K	+263 K	+725 K in Apr 1978	158 K	310	58.6%

serve call-ups. So these factors must be taken into account in interpreting the data, since many of these impacts are temporary and not associated with an improvement or worsening in the labor market.

The rapid rise of temporary help companies (such as Manpower, Kelly Services, etc.) during the 1980s has changed the payroll employment data. Historically, if a manufacturing firm hired a part-time worker, that person would be classified as a manufacturing worker. However, if that same manufacturer hired a worker through a temporary help company, that worker would be classified as a business service employee. This obviously changes the interpretation of the industry detail. Moreover, if that same temporary help firm employee works for two

FIGURE 9–4a Household Employment Changes

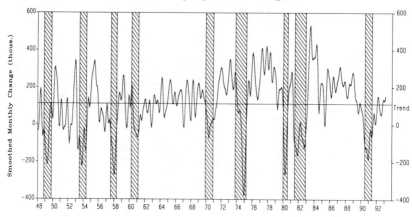

Note: Shaded areas represent business cycle recessions

FIGURE 9–4b Household Employment Changes
(January 1948–December 1992, Thousands of Jobs)

		Normal Bounds				Series Characteristics		
Period	Historic Low	Normal Low	Average	Normal High	Historic High	Standard Deviation	Share of Total Observations	
Recession	−761 K in Dec 1953	−236 K	−98 K	+40 K	+639 K in Feb 1954	276 K	96	18.1%
Recovery	−628 K in May 1991	+45 K	+185 K	+325 K	+991 K in Jun 1983	279 K	123	23.3%
Expansion	−947 K in Mar 1960	+5 K	+150 K	+295 K	+1286 K in Apr 1960	291 K	310	58.6%

firms on a part-time basis, that worker would be counted only once in the payroll employment report because that individual is working for only one temporary help company. This tends to eliminate some of the inevitable double-counting of workers that traditionally held multiple part-time jobs and has resulted in a downward bias in payroll employment growth.

Household employment by definition is not impacted by labor strikes or other temporary work disruptions. However, household employment changes tend to be much more volatile from month to month than the payroll series.

FIGURE 9–5a Unemployment Rate

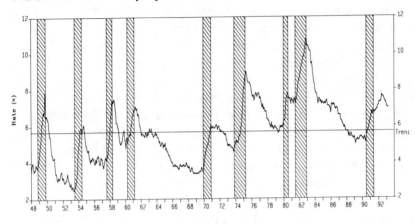

Note: Shaded areas represent business cycle recessions

FIGURE 9–5b Unemployment Rate
(January 1948–December 1992, Rate)

| Period | Historic Low | Normal Bounds | | | Historic High | Series Characteristics | |
		Normal Low	Average	Normal High		Standard Deviation	Share of Total Observations
Recession	2.7% in Aug 1953	5.5 %	6.3 %	7.2 %	10.8% in Nov 1982	1.7 pp	96	18.1%
Recovery	4.3% in May 1955	6.6 %	7.2 %	7.9 %	10.8% in Dec 1982	1.3 pp	123	23.3%
Expansion	2.5% in Jun 1953	4.5 %	5.1 %	5.8 %	7.5% in Sep 1992	1.3 pp	310	58.6%

Revisions

Because household employment data are based on a sample, they do not get revised on a monthly basis. However, once a year household employment data are adjusted to new annual employment benchmark levels and will include updated seasonal factors, which can marginally impact the month-to-month change.

On the other hand, payroll employment is revised twice after its initial release. The nonresponse rate for establishments is high for the initial estimate. The Labor Department only gets payroll data from about half of the 340,000 firms in time for the initial estimate. Although the half that does report accounts for substantially more than half of the total workforce, this rate of nonresponse is a major source of revision in these data. Even the federal government's own employment records are not available in time for the first estimate. The Office of Personnel Management (OPM) makes a preliminary estimate of federal government employment using an assumption of no employment change where records are not available. However, this OPM estimate is used only as a check against estimates of the number of federal government employments found on state employment records. Once each year, both the household and payroll measures of employment are benchmarked to more comprehensive data. The household revision is usually done with the March employment report while the payroll employment revision generally occurs with the May report. Payroll employment is adjusted or benchmarked for the March level of the prior year using unemployment insurance data (e.g., the May 1993 data revision was pegged to the March 1992 level of employment from the unemployment insurance reports).

Ongoing estimates of payroll employment are extrapolated by using a "link relative" method. From the March benchmark level of payroll employment, the Labor Department statisticians adjust future month's employment levels by a ratio of all employees in one month to all employees in the preceding month (the link relative) for the sample establishments that reported to the BLS in both months. To capture new business formations and its impact on new hirings, the BLS incorporates "bias" factors into their estimate of payroll employment. Those factors essentially gross up overall employment by a varying amount. Currently, the actual calculation of bias factors is based on a model tying the growth in employment of the rest of the sample.

Relationship with Other Series

The manufacturing hours data are used by the Federal Reserve Board in the derivation of their monthly industrial production series. Currently, the Federal Reserve receives this and only this subset of the employment data *ahead* of its initial release. Generally, it's the Wednesday before a Friday release of the employment data. These hours measures are directly part of the industrial production series.

Additionally, employee hours and earnings data are directly used by the Commerce Department in their derivation of the monthly personal income data. By statistical inference, construction employment data can be used as an indication of housing starts activity during the month (though the employment data is for one specific week—which could have been affected by adverse weather and may not be representative of the strength or weakness for the housing markets during the whole month). Similarly, total nonagricultural employee hours can be used as a proxy for quarterly GDP fluctuation. However, this relationship is tenuous because it assumes that the agricultural sector is relatively stable or insignificant (a fair assumption), that the output by the self-employed is relatively stable (unlikely), and that productivity is stable (a tough call).

References

Bureau of Labor Statistics, *BLS Handbook of Methods*, Bulletin 2285, 1988.

National Commission on Employment and Unemployment Statistics, *Counting the Labor Force*, 1979.

Chapter 10

Employment Cost Index

General Description

The employment cost index (ECI) is the one of the most comprehensive measures of labor costs. It includes both wages and benefits for state and local government and private sector employees. Wages and salaries account for about 72 percent of total labor costs, while the remaining 28 percent is benefits. The significance of the ECI has varied over time for the financial markets, given the overall concern with labor costs.

Economic Indicator Information at a Glance

Market Significance	Low-to-Moderate
Typical Release Time	10:00 AM Eastern Time Last Tuesday of First Month of New Quarter
Released By	Labor Department Bureau of Labor Statistics
Period Covered	Prior Quarter

Analyzing the Data

The ECI represents the price of labor as compensation per-employee hour worked and is measure for the pay period including the 12th day of the last month of each quarter (March, June, September, and December) using fixed-weight shares of labor. Self-employed, owner-managers, and unpaid family workers are excluded from the survey coverage. The wage and salary component of the ECI measures the average straight-time hourly earnings, where straight-time earnings are total earnings before deductions and excluding premium pay for overtime, weekend, or late-shift work. Earnings include production bonuses, commissions, and cost-of-living adjustments but exclude nonproduction bonuses such as payments in kind, room and board, and tips. On the benefit side, the ECI measures 23 distinct benefit categories:

Hours-Related Benefits:
1. Premium pay for overtime and work on holidays and weekends
2. Vacations
3. Holidays
4. Sick leave
5. Other paid leave

Supplemental Pay:
6. Shift differentials
7. Nonproduction bonuses
8. Severance pay
9. Supplemental unemployment benefit funds

Insurance:
10. Life insurance
11. Health benefits
12. Sickness and accident insurance

Pension and Savings Plans:
13. Pension and retirement benefits
14. Savings and thrift plans

Legally Required Benefits:
15. Social security
16. Railroad retirement
17. Railroad supplemental retirement
18. Railroad unemployment insurance
19. Federal Unemployment Tax Act
20. State unemployment insurance
21. Workers' compensation
22. Other legally required benefits

Merchandise Discounts:

23. Merchandise discounts (for retail trade employees only)

The ECI sample consists of about 4,400 private nonfarm establishments and 1,000 state and local government establishments. Federal government employees are not included in these data. Overtime pay is included in the benefits category with its appropriate fixed-weight share. Hence, an increase in the use of overtime by employers would not have any impact on the ECI, although it would increase the per worker labor costs actually paid by the employer.

In addition to the split in compensation between wage and salaries and benefits, the ECI also is compiled by: (1) occupational classes (professional, speciality, and technical; executive, administrative, and managerial; administration support; and blue-collar occupations), (2) type of industry (goods-producing and service-producing), (3) bargaining status (union or nonunion), (4) region (Northeast, South, Midwest, and West), and (5) area size (metropolitan areas or other).

The BLS began to seasonally adjust some of the major components and presents those on a quarter-to-quarter seasonally adjusted basis while other nonseasonally adjusted components continue to be presented and viewed on a year-over-year basis. (See Figures 10–1a and 10–1b.)

ECI over the Business Cycle

The short history of the ECI data makes cyclical analysis very tricky—especially given that there was a secular unwinding of inflation during the 1980s, which impacted these data. Over the last 10 years, the ECI has notched up 1.2 percent per quarter (on a quarter-to-quarter seasonally adjusted basis) with little discernible difference between recession, recovery, and expansion periods.

Special Factors, Limitations, and Other Data Issues

One of the key limitations of these data is the mixed presentation of seasonally adjusted and nonadjusted data, which makes

FIGURE 10–1a Employment Cost Index

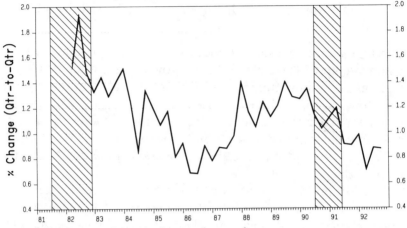

Note: Shaded areas represent business cycle recessions

FIGURE 10–1b Employment Cost Index
(1982 Q2–1992 Q4)

		Normal Bounds				Series Characteristics	
Period	Historic Low	Normal Low	Average	Normal High	Historic High	Standard Deviation	Share of Total Observations
Recession	+1.0% in 1990 Q4	+1.2%	+1.4%	+1.6%	+1.9% in 1982 Q2	0.4 pp.	4 | 10.3%
Recovery	+0.7% in 1992 Q2	+1.1%	+1.2%	+1.4%	+1.5% in 1984 Q1	0.3 pp.	10 | 25.6%
Expansion	+0.7% in 1986 Q3	+1.0%	+1.1%	+1.2%	+1.4% in 1989 Q3	0.2 pp.	25 | 64.1%

a detailed comparison difficult. But that detailed look might be appropriate in times of labor cost concern because regional labor cost rotations can be observed as well as the power of labor unions.

A second limitation of the data is that the ECI does not have an extension history; the ECI aggregate goes back to 1979, and more details were added over time. Hence, a complete cyclical review is not possible. Moreover, studies on other labor measures suggest that labor costs tend to be lagging economic indicators of the economy and the inflation cycle, which suggests that caution should be exercised in the cause-and-effect of a rise or fall in the ECI.

Relationship with Other Series

The average hourly earnings series, which is contained in the employment report, provides a monthly snapshot of wage costs. The financial markets are forced to review it since no other timely data exists. However, the ECI is conceptually superior to the average hourly earnings in terms of weighting and coverage. For example, the average hourly earnings data is impacted by changing employment shares from month to month, but the ECI is not. The average hourly earnings data does not account for irregular bonuses and excludes retroactive pay, as well as all employer-paid benefits and social security taxes, while the ECI accounts for those factors.

Reference

G. Donald Wood, "Employment Cost Index series to replace Hourly Earnings Index," *Monthly Labor Review*, July 1988, pp. 32–35.

Chapter 11

Federal Budget

General Description

The federal budget release tallies the U.S. Treasury's receipts and outlays. It is a rolling snapshot of the government's budget deficit; its importance to the financial markets is usually very limited.

Economic Indicator Information at a Glance

Market Significance	Low
Typical Release Time	2:00 PM Eastern Time Around the Fifteenth Business Day of the Month
Released By	Treasury Department, Financial Management Service
Period Covered	Prior Month

The U.S. government's fiscal year runs from October to September. Within a fiscal year, each month's result should be considered to be distinctly different from other months' results; there is a strong seasonality to monthly budget numbers. Thus, April's result should be compared with previous Aprils, not versus March or May results. The most obvious aspect of this seasonality is the months in which a budget surplus is likely or possible. These months are April, when final individual tax payments are due; and June, September, and December, when corporate tax receipts help create the potential for a surplus. April has continued to show a surplus even during the early 1990s, when budget deficits were reaching, what were then, all-time highs. The other months have not moved consistently into surplus, but they have at least shown a sharp decline in red ink relative to other months of the fiscal year.

Although there certainly are exceptions, volatility of the monthly budget numbers can be traced to the receipts side. Monthly receipts fluctuate as much as 100 percent, and in fiscal 1992 the average absolute month-to-month change was 39 percent. Expenditures, too, are variable, but the average absolute change was only 8.4 percent.

One final aspect of the federal budget is the usage of *on-budget* and *off-budget* totals. Off-budget items are receipts or outlays that are excluded from budget totals by law. The key components are the two Social Security trust funds and the Postal Service fund. The published federal budget numbers, and those cited in most analyses, combine both on- and off-budget results. In fiscal 1992 the total year's deficit was $290.2 bn., comprised of a $340.07 bn. on-budget deficit and a $49.9 bn. off-budget surplus. (See Figures 11-1 and 11-2.)

FIGURE 11-1 Federal Government Receipts
(July 1967–December 1992, Year/Year Percent Change)

		Normal Bounds				Series Characteristics	
Period	Historic Low	Normal Low	Average	Normal High	Historic High	Standard Deviation	Share of Total Observations
Recession	−10.2% in Oct 1982	1.4 %	5.4 %	9.5 %	+19.7% in Mar 1975	8.1 pp.	57	18.6%
Recovery	−33.5% in May 1975	−0.3 %	6.1 %	12.5 %	+77.3% in May 1976	12.7 pp.	83	27.1%
Expansion	−31.0% in Aug 1967	3.8 %	11.2 %	18.6 %	+83.0% in Jul 1968	14.8 pp.	166	54.2%

FIGURE 11-2 Federal Government Expenditures
(July 1967–December 1992, Year/Year Percent Change)

		Normal Bounds				Series Characteristics	
Period	Historic Low	Normal Low	Average	Normal High	Historic High	Standard Deviation	Share of Total Observations
Recession	−22.3% in Jan 1982	3.4 %	9.2 %	15.0 %	+39.4% in Dec 1974	11.6 pp.	75	16.4%
Recovery	−17.7% in Feb 1955	3.6 %	9.4 %	15.3 %	+59.6% in Sep 1980	11.7 pp.	109	23.9%
Expansion	−23.9% in Sep 1979	2.7 %	8.6 %	14.5 %	+62.9% in Apr 1968	11.8 pp.	272	59.6%

Analyzing the Data

An individual month's deficit usually carries little signifi-cance to financial markets. Even the fixed-income markets, whose literal existence or center of gravity (for corporate and mortgage back securities) is based on U.S. Treasury debt, find minimal trading value in the government's monthly accounting.

This is not to say that financial markets lack a deep concern about the size of the government's deficit. Any news that were to alter significantly the outlook for the deficit would have a dramatic effect on all financial markets. The passage of what is commonly called the Gramm-Rudman Act (see "Commonly Used Budget Terms") in late 1985 is a good example of how important deficit news can be to the markets. Although a fall in oil prices contributed to the constructive tone of the markets, long-term interest rates fell about 100-basis points between Oc-tober 1985, when the Gramm-Rudman Act was passed, and the end of the year. Stock prices also responded positively, rising a sharp 11.3 percent (S&P 500) in the final two months of the year.

The market's ambivalence to the monthly deficit numbers is because there is little value added in each month's tally. Fiscal year estimates of the deficit are made by the Office of Manage-ment and Budget and the Congressional Budget Office, and they are well known by market participants. Although these esti-mates change as the fiscal year progresses, it is a gradual proc-ess where one month's result is not likely to significantly affect the full year's tally. If there is one technical point to be aware of when the budget deficit is released, it is the effect the calendar can have on the expenditure side. Specifically, significant monthly payments are made by the government on the first three days of each month. Chief among them are Social Security transfer payments, retirement benefits, and payroll expendi-tures. If these days fall on a weekend or a holiday, the payments are pushed back to the prior business day. The most frequent occurrence is when the first of the month falls on a weekend or a holiday. Then the payments would be made on the final busi-ness day of the previous month, bloating the previous month's deficit and reducing the current month's number. The largest payments are Social Security disbursements that are made on the third of every month. Although unusual, it can happen that the first three days of a month fall on a combined weekend and

Commonly Used Budget Terms*

Balanced Budget Act

This is the Gramm-Rudman Act. It set specific deficit targets and enforceable sequestration procedures in the event the deficit targets were not adhered to.

Baseline Outlook

The standard against which one measures the effect that changes in revenue and expenditure legislation have on the budget. According to the Budget Enforcement Act of 1990 the baseline is built upon extant legislation remaining in place.

Budget Enforcement Act of 1990

This piece of legislation superseded the Balanced Budget Act and the Congressional Budget Act of 1974. It revised the deficit targets of the Balanced Budget Act and made them more flexible. It also established spending constraints under which increases above those allowed for in the act had to be matched by revenue increases or cuts in spending in specific areas. A similar offset is necessary for revenue reductions.

Budget Resolution

A resolution of the House and Senate that outlines Congress' budget plans for the next five years. It is not law. The resolution is put into effect via specific revenue and expenditure legislation.

Entitlements

Programs that make government payments based on recipients meeting specific requirements. Expenditures are controlled by Congress changing the requirements. These are often considered to be mandatory spending programs.

Standardized Employment Budget Deficit

The budget deficit that would exist, under then current law, if the economy were operating at its highest, noninflationary rate of growth.

*This section draws heavily from the Congressional Budget Office's Glossary of Terms included in its annual Economic and Budget Outlook. For a more extensive list of budget terms, please consult this glossary.

holiday. In those instances, the effect on the monthly deficit can cause a swing in the deficit of close to $30 bn.

Government Finances over the Cycle

The cyclicality of the federal budget deficit is very strong, and it is especially noticeable during recessions. Then the deficit increases sharply. This pronounced change is most evident on the receipt side. The average year-to-year increase in federal government receipts is only 5.4 percent, compared to 6.1 percent in the recovery and 11.2 percent during the expansion. The markedly different rate of growth for receipts during the expansion is as much accounted for by higher inflation rates, which bloat nominal tax receipts, as by the rate of economic activity. Expenditures show much less of a cyclical pattern. In fact, the average growth of expenditures is slightly greater during recoveries (+9.4 percent) than during recessions (+9.2 percent). This is accounted by the fact that unemployment is a lagging indicator, and benefits associated with this type of spending spill into the recovery phase. (See Figures 11–1 and 11–2.)

Chapter 12

Gross Domestic Product

General Description

The National Income and Product Accounts, which is the formal name for the Gross Domestic Product (GDP) report, are the hallmark of the Commerce Department's effort to provide a comprehensive accounting of final demand. Built as a system of interlocking sector accounts, the GDP report provides the most comprehensive reading of the nation's health. These quarterly data, which are revised on a monthly basis, are expressed in annualized growth-rate terms (see page 88) with the sole exception of the corporate profits data, which, because of their volatility, are not annualized and are only expressed on a quarter-to-quarter percentage change basis.

Economic Indicator Information at a Glance

Market Significance	Very High for Initial Estimate of Quarter but Progressively Less Important for Revisions
Typical Release Time	8:30 AM Eastern Time About 20th Business Day
Released By	Commerce Department Bureau of Economic Analysis
Month Covered	Prior Quarter

Analyzing the Data

The GDP report can be thought of as two estimates for real GDP (which are constrained to be equal). The first estimate is built from the final demand categories such as consumption (C), investment (I), government spending (G), and net exports (NE). A second estimate is built from the income side, which includes personal income (PI) and profits (PR). In its most basic form:

$$GDP = C + I + G + NE = PI + PR$$

Although that is the theory, there are numerous refinements to this basic identity in practice, and a statistical discrepancy is added to the income side to force equality between the two measurement approaches. The relationship between the income and product sides of the account ledger is shown in Figure 12–1. In 1991, for example, personal consumption expenditures accounted for 68.5 percent of nominal GDP, which was the largest single product account category, while compensation of employees accounted for 59.7 percent of nominal GDP, which was the largest component on the income ledger.

The first estimate of real GDP for the prior quarter is released about 20 business days after the end of the quarter. Subsequent to the first estimate, the quarterly data are revised twice over the next two months. Generally, in July real GDP data are revised to include benchmark revisions to the underlying source data, minor methodology improvements, and new seasonal factors. The mid-year data revisions extend back three years. More comprehensive revisions occur less frequently, and those revisions could extend back to 1929, when the annual data series starts.

The keys to interpreting the national income report follow:

- Separately view the real GDP growth as final sales and inventory change. If the change in inventories was large, then ask yourself whether it was more likely involuntary or voluntary accumulation or decumulation. The answer to that question could have significant implication for future growth prospects.
- Keep an eye on the savings rate. Recognize, however, that the savings rate is conceptually faulty, since the savings rate methodology assumes that the entire purchase price of a car, for example, is offset against disposable income in the current period instead of the monthly payment for

the item. But still, it provides a benchmark for determining how strong or weak future consumption might be.

- Look at real gross domestic purchases as well as real GDP. Domestic purchases measure how strong domestic demand is regardless of the source of the demand (domestic or foreign). For example, a strong gain in real domestic purchases but a weak gain in real GDP suggests that imports are sapping off a lot of demand. This leads to the question of whether policy makers are content about the foreign exchange value of the dollar.
- Do not be too concerned with changes in the implicit price deflator; instead, focus upon the fixed-weight price index—which holds shares of GDP constant and provides a better gauge of overall inflation. In most cases, this is old news anyway because inflation can be tracked on a monthly basis from the CPI, PPI, and import/export price data.
- Separately look at the pace of exports and imports. Have they strengthened or weakened? Is the nominal trade deficit dramatically different from the real deficit? If so, that might suggest the impact changes in the foreign exchange value of the dollar.
- How strong is real capital spending? Take a look at nominal spending as well since declining computer prices could have a big impact on pushing up the real value of spending.
- Finally, especially for the equity markets, take a look at net cashflow—which is calculated from corporate profits. A strong increase or a sharp decline in net cashflow has implications for credit borrowing needs of companies.

Real GDP over the Business Cycle

To understand fluctuation in real GDP and its components, it is useful to think of growth as determined by *secular* or *long-term factors*, such as demographics, the end of the Cold War, and so forth; and cyclical factors, such as temporary interruptions in growth due to shocks or other maladjustments in the economy. Between 1947 and 1992, real GDP growth expanded at an average annualized rate of 3.1 percent per quarter, and that pace

FIGURE 12–1 The Product and Income Measures of GDP

(For 1991, Billions of Current Dollars)

Product		Income	
Personal Consumption Expenditures	$3,887.7	Compensation of Employees	$3,390.8
Durable Goods	446.1	Wages and Salaries	2,812.2
Nondurable Goods	1,251.5	Supplements to Wages and Salaries	578.7
Services	2,190.1	Proprietors' Income (with Adjustments)	368.0
Gross Private Domestic Investment	721.1	Farm	35.8
Fixed Investment	731.3	Nonfarm	332.2
Nonresidential	541.1	Rental Income of Persons (with Adjustments)	-10.4
Structures	180.1	Corporate Profits (with Adjustments)	346.3
Producers' Durable Equipment	360.9	Profits before Taxes	334.7
Residential	190.3	Inventory Valuation Adjustment	3.1
Change in Inventories	-10.2	Capital Consumption Adjustment	8.4
Nonfarm	-10.3	Net Interest	449.5
Farm	0.0	Miscellaneous Adjustments	1,133.3
Net Exports of Goods and Services	-21.8	Net National Product Adjustments	524.6
Exports	598.2	Depreciation Adjustments	626.1
Imports	620.0	Net Receipts of Factor Income Adjustment	-17.4
Government Purchases	1,090.5		
Federal	447.3		
National Defense	323.8		
Nondefense	123.6		
State and Local	643.2		
Gross Domestic Product	5,677.5	Gross Domestic Product	5,677.5

notched lower by only 0.2 percentage points to 2.9 percent per quarter over the last 10 years (see Figure 12–2). Two secular reasons for that slowdown are a slower growing prime consumer-aged population and better inventory control, indeed, the pace of nonfarm inventories showed a dramatic slowdown over that period. For the 1947–1992 period, nonfarm inventories grew roughly in lock-step with final sales. However, in the 1983–92 period, inventories grew considerably less than the pace of final sales, as shown in Figure 12–3.

Figures 12–4a and 12–4b present the specific cycle contractions and rebounds in real GDP during the postwar period along with their duration. In the nine business cycle contractions during that period, the average annual decline was 3.4

Gross Domestic Product   83

FIGURE 12–2 Real GDP and Inventories

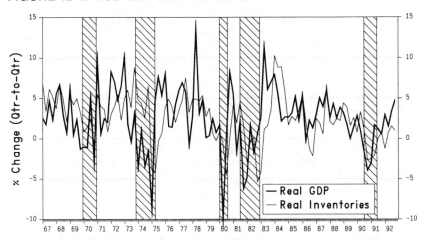

Note: Shaded areas represent business cycle recessions.

FIGURE 12–3 Growth in Real GDP and Its Components

| | Average Growth Rates | | | | | |
| | | Normal Bounds | | | Normal Bounds | |
	1974–92	Low	High	1983–92	Low	High
Real GDP	3.1%	1.5%	4.6%	2.9%	1.9%	3.9%
Final Sales	3.1	1.8	4.4	2.8	1.7	3.9
Consumption	3.2	2.0	4.4	2.9	1.9	4.0
Producers' Durable Equipment	3.4	-2.3	9.1	4.7	0.5	8.9
Nonresidential Structures	2.4	-1.9	6.7	-1.7	-7.1	3.7
Residential Structures	2.6	-6.3	11.5	4.5	-2.3	11.4
Federal Government Spending	2.7	-2.0	7.4	1.8	-1.4	4.9
State and Local Government Spending	3.7	2.2	5.2	3.0	2.1	3.9
Exports	4.4	-2.5	11.3	7.5	4.6	10.4
Imports	6.3	-0.3	13.0	7.8	3.4	12.2
Inventories	3.0	1.5	4.4	2.1	0.9	3.2
Nonfarm Inventories	3.2	1.7	4.8	2.5	1.2	3.8

Note: Normal bounds are the geometric average growth rate plus or minus one-half of the average absolute deviation from the mean.

FIGURE 12–4a Business Cycle Recessions and Recoveries

Amplitude and Speed of Business Recoveries based on Real GDP

U.S Recessions	RECESSIONS				RECOVERIES				Speed of Rebound*
	Annual Rate % Decline	Number of Qtrs.	Cumulative % Decline	% Change Per Period	Annual Rate % Rebound	Number of Qtrs.	Cumulative % Rebound	% Change Per Period	
1948–49	−1.1	4	−1.1	−0.3	15.9	1	3.8	3.8	13.7
1953–54	−2.2	4	−2.2	−0.5	4.9	2	2.4	1.2	2.2
1957–58	−6.5	2	−3.3	−1.7	6.8	3	5.1	1.7	1.0
1960–61	−1.1	3	−0.8	−0.3	3.4	1	0.8	0.8	3.1
1969–70	−1.2	3	−0.9	−0.3	5.1	1	1.2	1.2	4.3
1973–75	−3.3	5	−4.1	−0.8	5.9	3	4.4	1.5	1.8
1980	−9.9	1	−2.6	−2.6	4.6	3	3.4	1.1	0.4
1981–82	−2.8	4	−2.8	−0.7	4.7	3	3.5	1.2	1.6
1990–91	−2.9	3	−2.2	−0.7	1.9	6	2.9	0.5	0.7
Average: 1948–1991	−3.4	3.2	−2.2	−0.9	5.9	2.6	3.1	1.4	3.2
Median: 1948–1991	−2.8		−2.2	−0.7	4.9		3.4	1.2	2.2

*The "speed of rebound" statistic is calculated as the per period rebound in real GDP (on its specific cycle) to the previous peak divided by the per period contraction in real GDP.

FIGURE 12–4b Business Cycle Recoveries and Expansions

Amplitude and Speed of Business Expansions based on Real GDP

U.S Expansions	Recovery & Expansion				EXPANSION				Speed of Change*
	Annual Rate % Gain	Number of Qtrs.	Cumulative % Increase	% Change Per Period	Annual Rate % Gain	Number of Qtrs.	Cumulative % Rebound	% Change Per Period	
1949–53	7.8	14	30.2	2.2	7.2	13	25.5	2.0	0.52
1954–57	3.4	13	11.6	0.9	3.2	11	9.0	0.8	0.68
1958–60	5.1	8	10.4	1.3	4.1	5	5.1	1.0	0.60
1961–69	4.5	35	47.1	1.3	4.5	34	45.9	1.3	1.62
1970–73	4.1	14	15.0	1.1	4.0	13	13.6	1.0	0.84
1975–80	4.0	20	21.5	1.1	3.6	17	16.3	1.0	0.66
1980–81	2.8	5	3.5	0.7	0.2	2	0.1	0.1	0.05
1982–90	3.5	31	30.6	1.0	3.4	28	26.1	0.9	0.80
Average: 1948–1991	4.4	17.5	21.2	1.2	3.8	15.4	17.7	1.0	0.72
Median: 1948–1991	4.3		18.3	1.1	3.8		15.0	1.0	

*The "speed of change" statistic is calculated as the per period increase in real GDP (on its specific cycle basis) from when it "returned to previous peak" divided by cumulative rebound.

percent, with the smallest decline of 1.1 percent in 1948 and 1960 and the largest decline in 1980, with an annualized decline of 9.9 percent. The average length of a recession lasted three quarters. On a cumulative basis, the largest decline in real GDP occurred during the 1973–1975 recession.

During the rebound phase of the cycle, real growth tends to expand at a 5.9 percent pace, on average, and then settle down to a 3.8 percent growth rate during the expansion phase. However, the 1990–1991 rebound was substantially weaker than the average experience due to secular forces in the economy, while the 1948–1949 rebound was substantially stronger than the average. The slow rebound from 1990–1991 recession is clear from

the "speed of rebound" statistic shown in Figure 12–4a. However, as a generalization, the sharper the contraction, the sharper
the rebound, but there are some major exceptions.

Another business cycle generalization is that the sharper the
rebound in the economy following a recession, the stronger the
annualized trend pace of real GDP growth over the remainder
of the business cycle expansion. This relationship is shown by
the estimated relationship in Figure 12–5.

Special Factors, Limitations, and Other Data Issues

One of the most perplexing questions for policy makers is:
"what is the relationship between the unemployment rate and
real GDP growth?" In the early 1960s, this gave rise to an infa-
mous law by Arthur Okun, who later became Chairman of
President Johnson's Council of Economic Advisers. Okun's Law,
which was later rescinded by Okun, continues to be held by the
economics profession and can be formulated in a slightly different form then Okun originally formulated it. Between 1980–1992
or between 1985–1992, the estimated rule of thumb suggests that
real GDP has to grow by 2.2 percent for the unemployment rate
to remain unchanged. If real GDP growth was 1 percent
stronger than that threshold level, then the unemployment rate

**FIGURE 12–5 Estimating the Trend Pace of Real GDP Growth
During Expansions Based on the Strength of the Rebound from
the Prior Contraction**

Expansion Growth = 1.5 + 0.35 × Rebound Amplitude			
Expansions	Actual Growth	Predicted	Error
1949–53	7.2%	7.1%	0.1 pp.*
1954–57	3.2	3.2	0.0
1958–60	4.1	3.9	0.2
1961–69	4.5	2.7	1.8
1970–73	4.0	3.3	0.7
1975–80	3.6	3.6	0.0
1980–81	0.2	3.1	−2.9
1982–90	3.4	3.2	0.2
1991–	—	2.2	—

*percentage points

would tend to decline by 0.1 percentage point per quarter and vice versa.

Another concept that is often heard at Congressional committee testimony is *potential real GDP*. Although the derivation of potential output is open to debate, the Congressional Budget Office has institutionalized the concept. Potential real GDP is the maximum attainable level of output that could exist without putting upward pressure on inflation. The derivation of the concept incorporates a concept known as NAIRU—the nonaccelerating inflation rate of unemployment—which in 1992 was thought to be 5.5 percent. When the actual unemployment rate—which was 7.4 percent in 1992—approaches the NAIRU, then economists tend to worry that inflation will heat up.

Relationship with Other Series

The GDP data are used in the Federal Reserve's Flow-of-Funds (FOF) data accounting structure, but certain concepts are redefined on an FOF basis. One of the most interesting conceptual differences is the treatment of personal savings, where the FOF definition of savings adjusts for consumer spending flows and not total purchase price. The prime example of this difference is with car purchases. On the national income account (NIA) definition, a car that is purchased in a given period is assumed to be current consumption while the FOF concept only assumes that the car service (not the total purchase price) during that period represents current consumption. As such, the FOF personal savings rate is considerably higher than that reported by the Commerce Department. In 1991, for example, the NIA measure of the personal savings rate was 4.7 percent while the FOF measure was 8.0 percent. Although it is more important to look at the relative shifts in each series over time to evaluate the importance of a rise or decline in savings, even this can produce different impressions, such as between 1984 and 1985 (see Figure 12–6).

FIGURE 12–6 Two Measures of the Personal Savings Rate
(Personal Savings as a Percent of Disposable Personal Income)

	'80	'81	'82	'83	'84	'85	'86	'87	'88	'89	'90	'91	'92
FOF Measure	10.9	10.9	11.3	12.5	13.9	12.2	13.9	10.3	10.7	12.0	10.3	8.5	9.1
NIA Measure	7.9	8.8	8.6	6.8	8.0	6.4	6.0	4.3	4.4	4.0	4.3	4.7	4.8

References

Carson, Carol S. and George Jaszi, *The Use of National Income and Product Accounts for Public Policy: Our Successes and Failures*, Staff Paper 43, U.S. Department of Commerce, January 1986.

Corporate Profits: Profits before Taxes, Profits Tax Liability, and Dividends, U.S. Department of Commerce, Washington, D.C., 1985.

Foreign Transactions, U.S. Department of Commerce, Washington D.C., 1987.

GNP: *Overview of Source Data and Estimating Methods* , U.S. Department of Commerce, Washington, D.C., 1987.

Government Transactions, U.S. Department of Commerce, Washington, D.C., 1988.

Introduction to National Economic Accounting, U.S. Department of Commerce, Washington, D.C., 1985.

Personal Consumption Expenditures, U.S. Department of Commerce, Washington, D.C., 1990.

Webb, Roy H., "The National Income and Product Accounts," *Macroeconomic Data: A User's Guide*, Federal Reserve Bank of Richmond, 1990, pp. 7–13.

Calculating an Annualized Growth Rate

The convention used to express GDP growth rate changes is to annualize the quarterly growth rate, and that is calculated as follows:

$$rate = ((GDP\ [current\ period]/GDP\ [prior\ period])^4 - 1) \times 100$$

where the current and prior period data is in level terms (billions of dollars). For example, if the third quarter level of real GDP was $4,933.7 billion and the fourth quarter level was $4,972.7 billion, then the annualized rate of change would be:

$$(($4972.7\ /\ $4933.7)^4 - 1) \times 100 = ((1.008^4) - 1) \times 100 = (1.032 - 1) \times 100 = 3.2\%$$

Economists generally express the annual growth rate as the current year's fourth quarter over the prior year's fourth quarter (Q4/Q4) as a way of measuring change within the year. The alternative would be to average growth rates* during the year, which is not generally done.

The Q4/Q4 growth rates can be substantially different from the calendar-year annual growth rate. It is even possible to have a very different impression viewing growth on a Q4/Q4 basis versus calendar-year average growth. For example, the 1981 calendar-year real GDP growth was 1.8 percent, while the 1981 Q4/Q4 growth rate was -0.1 percent.

*Technically, the average must be a geometric average; otherwise, an arithmetic average (the "simple average") would create a mathematical bias.

Glossary of Key National Income Terms

Output and Price Measures

Gross National Product: GNP measures the output of the residents of the United States.

Gross Domestic Product: In 1991, the Commerce Department shifted its focus from real GNP to real GDP. GDP measures the value of items produced within the borders of the United States.

Gross Domestic Purchases: This is a measure of domestic demand—regardless of whether demand is met from a foreign source; it is defined as gross domestic product less net exports.

Command-Basis GNP: Command-basis real GNP arose out of a conceptual problem in deflating imports and exports separately. For example, if the foreign exchange value of the dollar declined and import prices rise faster than export prices, then that could boost reported output. To counter this problem, the Commerce Department publishes a measure of real GNP that deflates exports and imports by the same implicit price deflator for imports.

Fixed-Weight Price Index: To better reflect inflation changes aside from compositional changes, the Commerce Department calculates a fixed-weight price index. As the name implies, the shares of various sectors are held constant so as to measure price changes alone.

Implicit Price Deflator: The Commerce Department has been downplaying the implicit price deflators for quite some time. Although they measure price change, they are biased by shifts in the value of output. For example, if capital spending soars in a given period and capital spending has very low sector inflation relative to other components of the NIA accounts, this will cause the implicit price deflator to slow more than otherwise due to the output shift to a lower inflation sector.

Through the Profit Maze

Overview: Which measure of profitability is most important? According to our analysis, it all depends on your purpose. But the simple answer is that pretax corporate profits is the best national income and product accounts (NIPA) indicator of shareholder earnings growth, while the operating profits measure is the best indicator of stock price growth. Here is a list of terms and a figure (see Figure 12–7) to put the measures into perspective.

Profits from Current Production: This measure, also known as corporate profits with inventory valuation adjustment (IVA) and capital consumption adjustment (CCAdj) or sometimes referred to as "pretax economic profits" or "operating profits," is corporate profits before taxes and generally is net of company receipts and expenses as defined by federal tax law. The main differences between the national income account (NIA) concept and the treatment under federal tax laws are: (1) NIA receipts exclude capital gains and dividends received, (2) NIA expenses exclude depletion and capital loss, (3) NIA inventories are valued at replacement cost, and (4) NIA depreciation is adjusted for consistent accounting practices and valued at current replacement cost. By definition: profits from current production equals pretax profits plus IVA plus CCAdj.

Corporate Profits with IVA: This measure is similar to profits from current production except it reflects depreciation accounting methods used for federal tax returns. Industry profits are shown this way because industry capital consumption adjustments are not available.

Pretax Profits: This measure also is known as "book profits" and represents profits used in federal income tax returns. It equals the sum of taxes, dividends, and retained earnings.

Profits Tax Liability: This is the tax liability paid to all governmental units (federal, state, and local) on corporate income. These taxes are calculated on an accrual basis.

Profits after Tax: This is pretax profits minus profit tax liabilities.

Dividends: These are payments in cash or other assets, excluding the corporation's own stock, made to U.S. residents from domestic and foreign companies. These payments excluded dividends received by U.S. corporations.

Undistributed Corporate Profits: This measure is more commonly referred to as "retained earnings" and is pretax profits minus taxes and dividends.

Inventory Valuation Adjustment (IVA): This is the difference between the cost of inventories as recorded in federal tax returns and inventories valued at current replacement cost.

Capital Consumption Adjustment (CCAdj): This adjustment converts depreciation as recorded for tax purposes to a consistent accounting basis valued at current replacement cost.

Shareholder Profits: Corporate earnings such as those aggregate measures reported by the Standard & Poor's or Dow Jones' composites are operating profits minus depreciation, taxes, and nonoperating expenses as recorded in company income statements.

Economic Profits: This measure is after-tax profits plus IVA plus CCAdj.

Net Cashflow with Adjustments: This measure equals depreciation plus retained earnings with IVA and CCAdj and represents an internally generated source of funds for business, which would be supplemented by external financing (mainly from funds raised in the credit markets). A large increase (or decrease) in internal funds will tend to create less (or more) borrowing by business, assuming businesses face a steady demand for funds to fund capital expenditures and inventories.

FIGURE 12–7 Evaluating National Income Measures of Corporate Profitability

Profit Measure	Economic Significance	Relationship with Stockholder Earnings	Relative		Relationship with Stock Prices	Relative	
			Score	Rank		Score	Rank
(1) "Operating" Profit	Best gauge of profits from current production	Ranked as third lowest	58	4	Best gauge of stock prices	100	1
(2) Pretax Profit	Measures income from current production but includes "paper" inventory profits	Best gauge of stockholder earnings of the six measures evaluated	100	1	Relationship weakens sharply, in third place	27	3
(3) Aftertax Profits	Same as pretax profits but excludes tax payments	Close runner-up for best performance, with second highest score	97	2	Extremely weak relationship with stock prices	7	6
(4) Economic Profits	Same as operating profits but excludes tax payments	Ranked as second lowest	30	5	Second best measure to watch	84	2
(5) Net Cashflow	Conceptually, the best indicator of future capital spending	Lowest relationship with stockholder earnings	21	6	Ranked in fourth place	20	4
(6) Real Aftertax Profits	Same as aftertax profits but adjusted for inflation	In third place, but still quite high	94	3	A low fifth place reading	16	5

Note: Scoring system based on best correlation between National Income and Product Accounts (NIPA) profit measures and shareholder earnings and stock prices based on the S&P 500 and calculated on a year-over-year percentage change basis from 1960-1992. The series with the highest explanatory power was set equal to 100 (an arbitrary scale); all other series are ranked by their relative performance to the highest one.

Chapter 13

Home Sales: New One-Family and Existing

New One-Family Home Sales

General Description: The new one-family home sales series is derived directly from the housing starts data. It is presented in a seasonally adjusted, annualized data format. Commerce Department field representatives continuously followup on the individual starts information, from the structure's inception to its completion. Then, it is catalogued as being for sale, having been sold, or having been built by the landowner. A sale is defined as the signing of the initial contract to purchase a structure. A home built by and for owner use is not classified as a sale.

New one-family home sales account for about 15 percent of

Economic Indicator Information at a Glance

Market Significance	Low-to-Moderate
Typical Release Time	10:00 AM Eastern Time End of the Month
Released By	Commerce Dept./HUD
Period Covered	One Month Prior

the home sales market. Along with the existing home sales data provided by the National Association of Realtors (NAR), they fill out the other side of the housing market. Housing starts show us the building response and sales the purchasing response. Conceptually, builders will not build unless they see demand, and they will keep building if demand holds up, so home sales should be considered the initial step in the housing market's reaction to interest rate changes. Home sales also are a very good leading indicator of consumption, particularly durable goods purchases.

A casual glance at the two series reveals an obvious discrepancy between the housing starts levels and home sales levels. At a time when single-family starts may be running between 700,000 and 900,000 units, single-family sales may register only in the 400,000 to 600,000 range. Clearly, some of the starts wind up in the for-sale category, while the remaining difference is due to those homes that were built by the landowner for rental purposes or for the owner's own use.

The home sales data are broken down only one way—into four regions, Northeast, South, Midwest, and West. Also provided is the month's supply of houses for sale. This statistic is often used to forecast the housing starts series. The new home sales series is reasonably reliable and not nearly as susceptible to weather-related influences as are housing starts. Wet or cold weather can physically delay a start, but should have less impact on one's purchase of a home.

Existing Home Sales

General Description: The existing home sales series is compiled by the NAR—not a government agency. The monthly existing home sales data are collected by the NAR from a national sample of 125 multiple-listing realtors. Quarterly data, which offers a state-by-state breakdown, is taken from a sample of 600 realtors. The monthly data is broken down into the same four regions as the housing starts and new homes sales data. The quarterly data is available on a state-by-state breakdown. Existing home sales account for about 85 percent of the home sales market; therefore, they are a critical picture of the health of the consumer, although this series has only lately entered into the market's conscience. New home sales always were considered the more important of the two statistics because they lead directly to new starts and stronger economic activity. However, existing home sales are a much better indicator of consumption trends than are new home sales, given their huge share of the home sales market.

Economic Indicator Information at a Glance

Market Significance	Low-to-Moderate
Typical Release Time	8:45 AM Eastern Time 25th or First Business Day Thereafter
Released By	National Association of Realtors
Period Covered	One Month Prior

The key difference between the new home sales and existing home sales data is the definition of a sale. The existing home sales data is a combination of sales being registered at time of signing of the initial contract and of the final closing being considered the sale. Fully 60 percent of the existing home sales data is based on closings. The result is a series that lags the new home sales series, making it a bit less timely of a indicator of cyclical peaks and troughs than the new homes sales data.

The cyclical nature of home sales data is rather strong, as one would expect from such an interest rate sensitive sector. In each cycle since the 1960s, when the data begin, both new home sales and existing home sales have led the overall business cycle. However, the consistency of the lead time is greater for the trough than the peak. New home sales have peaked anywhere from eight to four quarters before the top of the total business cycle. Existing home sales have a slightly narrower range of four to six quarters. And the two peaks do not typically align, only having done so once since the two series began. Their troughs, however, align three out of four times, and both have a lead time of only one to three quarters.

Analyzing the Data

The analysis of the data for both series is again based on the breadth and depth of the change. The more widespread the overall change across the four regions, the more credibility the result has with analysts and the financial markets. One can also

FIGURE 13–1a New Home Sales

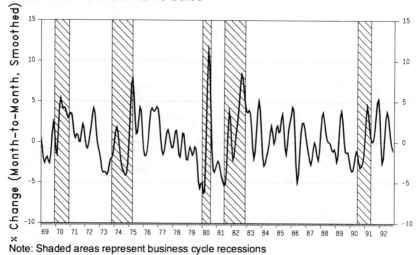

Note: Shaded areas represent business cycle recessions

FIGURE 13–1b New Home Sales
(February 1963–December 1992, Percent Change)

		Normal Bounds				Series Characteristics	
Period	Historic Low	Normal Low	Average	Normal High	Historic High	Standard Deviation	Share of Total Observations
Recession	−21.9% in Apr 1980	−4.2 %	1.1 %	6.4 %	+26.8% in May 1980	10.5 pp.	57	15.9%
Recovery	−12.1% in Mar 1992	−2.0 %	1.3 %	4.6 %	+20.0% in Dec 1983	6.5 pp.	83	23.1%
Expansion	−21.5% in Feb 1963	−4.0 %	−0.2 %	3.6 %	+31.2% in Apr 1963	7.5 pp.	219	61.0%

compare the behavior of the two series to ensure consistency in the picture of the housing market being painted. The two home sales series do not suffer from as much volatility as the housing starts data, but they suffer nevertheless. Under the circumstances, a trend analysis of the data is crucial in understanding one month's result and putting it in its proper perspective.

Home Sales over the Cycle

New and existing home sales show slightly different cyclical patterns. New home sales tend to follow the interest rate cycle. They are strong during recessions as they lead the economy out of the downturn. The average pace of growth picks up only marginally during the recovery stage. By the expansion phase, the good times are over for the new home sector, with the aver-

FIGURE 13–2a Existing Home Sales

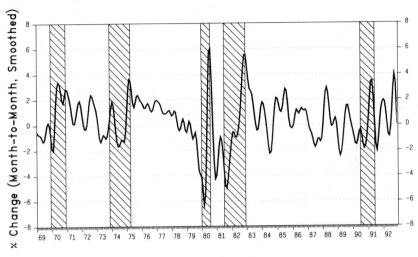

Note: Shaded areas represent business cycle recessions

FIGURE 13–2b Existing Home Sales
(February 1968–December 1992, Percent Change)

		Normal Bounds				Series Characteristics	
Period	Historic Low	Normal Low	Average	Normal High	Historic High	Standard Deviation	Share of Total Observations
Recession	−14.5% in Apr 1980	−2.7 %	−0.1 %	2.5 %	+12.7% in Jul 1980	5.2 pp.	57	19.1%
Recovery	−6.9% in Jan 1981	−0.6 %	1.2 %	3.0 %	+13.2% in Jan 1983	3.5 pp.	83	27.8%
Expansion	−10.5% in Jan 1987	−1.5 %	0.2 %	1.9 %	+12.4% in Dec 1986	3.3 pp.	159	53.2%

age month-to-month change for sales actually declining during expansions. Existing home sales follow the business cycle. On average, they decline during recessions, grow strongest during recoveries, and show marginal gains during the expansion phase. (See Figures 13–1a, 13–1b, 13–2a, and 13–2b.)

Chapter 14

Housing Starts and Building Permits

General Description

The *housing starts* release is one of the two most important looks at the residential housing sector; this one comes from the building side. Although the release is usually of moderate interest to the financial markets, its importance rises around turning points in the business cycle. Given the housing sector's interest sensitivity, starts should be one of the first sectors to suffer the ill effects of rising interest rates or the positive effects of falling interest rates. Significant reactions of starts and permits to changing interest rates is likely to be one of the first signals that the interest rate cycle is nearing its trough or peak. In this regard, building permits are one of the components of the leading economic indicators composite index.

Economic Indicator Information at a Glance

Market Significance	Moderate
Typical Release Time	8:30 AM Eastern Time Close to the Fifteenth Business Day of the Month
Released By	Commerce Department, Census Bureau
Period Covered	One Month Prior

The number is released as a seasonally adjusted annualized rate of the number of residential housing units started in a given month. Commerce Department field representatives, after first receiving permit information, survey building sites to determine actual starts. The sample survey consists of 844 permit sites (local, county, and state building permit offices) out of 17,000 potential sites.

Building permits are a separate survey. Without the need to survey building sites, it is possible for all 17,000 source information sites to be included in the permit survey.

The single-family housing starts data is one of the inputs into the calculation of the residential investment component of GDP, although it is not the key one.

Both starts and permits are broken down two ways: by the number of housing units per foundation and the regions in which they occurred. The unit categories are one (single-family residence), two to four, and five or more. The latter two categories are analytically grouped together and called the *multi-family sector.* The regional breakdown is Northeast, South, Midwest, and West. The single-family sector is the bulk of the starts and permits data on a level basis. Typically, single-family starts account for about 85 percent of total starts and single-family permits account for about 82 percent of the reported total. However, the multi-family sector typically contributes much of the volatility to the release. For example, in 1992 (a typical year) single-family permits and starts averaged changes (in absolute terms) of 5.7 percent and 3.1 percent, respectively, while multi-family starts and permits came in at an average of 23.9 percent and 7.5 percent, respectively.

Although financial market participants still insist upon viewing building permits as a leading indicator of housing activity, it is worth noting that this relationship is useful only for the multi-family sector. For single-family starts, at least two-thirds of the necessary permits are taken out in the same month as the actual start.

Analyzing the Data

Given the limited detail of the release, interpretation of the data is rather straightforward. The financial markets typically

FIGURE 14–1a Housing Starts

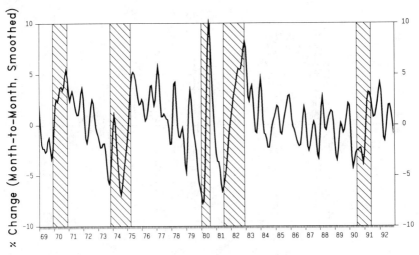

Note: Shaded areas represent business cycle recessions

FIGURE 14–1b Housing Starts
(January 1959–December 1992, Units)

Period	Historic Low	Normal Bounds			Historic High	Series Characteristics		
		Normal Low	Average	Normal High		Standard Deviation	Share of Total Observations	
Recession	819 K in Jan 1991	1059 K	1174 K	1288 K	1752 K in Feb 1974	229 K	67	16.4%
Recovery	982 K in May 1991	1366 K	1540 K	1714 K	2494 K in Jan 1972	348 K	96	23.5%
Expansion	843 K in Oct 1966	1445 K	1602 K	1759 K	2485 K in Oct 1972	314 K	245	60.0%

focus on the overall percentage change in the level of housing starts and building permits from the previous month. From there, it's necessary to break down the change into the single and multi sectors. Since the single-family sector dominates the residential housing market in terms of economic activity, the change in this sector is of more fundamental economic importance to analysts and the markets. This is the sector that tells the markets whether or not buyers and builders are responding to changing fundamentals, particularly interest rates. Multi-family starts and permits are a less reliable guide to fundamentals. Tax issues, both local and national, can play as large a role in determining this sector's behavior as can economic activity.

FIGURE 14–2a Building Permits

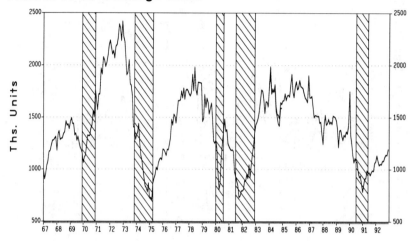

Note: Shaded areas represent business cycle recessions

FIGURE 14–2b Building Permits
(January 1984–December 1992, Units)

Period	Historic Low	Normal Bounds			Historic High	Series Characteristics		
		Normal Low	Average	Normal High		Standard Deviation	Share of Total Observations	
Recession	786 K in Jan 1991	872 K	915 K	958 K	1069 K in Aug 1990	86 K	8	7.4%
Recovery	916 K in Apr 1983	1011 K	1176 K	1341 K	1987 K in Feb 1984	330 K	21	19.4%
Expansion	1067 K in May 1990	1416 K	1525 K	1633 K	1916 K in Sep 1985	217 K	79	73.1%

The second level of analysis is the regional breakdown. In particular, the breadth of the change is critical to interpretation. An increase/decrease that is spread across all four regions carries much more analytical weight and is more believable than one that is concentrated solely in one region. Revisions to previous month's data can be a significant factor in analyzing the release.

Housing starts and permits data are unusually susceptible to weather influences. Awareness of precipitation levels around the country (a data publication is offered by the National Weather Service) can be an invaluable tool in analyzing (and forecasting) this release. Each series is also extremely volatile.

Analysis of one month's outcome must always be done in the context of what each series has done in the previous month and the most recent three-month average.

Housing Starts and Building Permits over the Business Cycle

Both starts and permits show a clear, strong cyclical bias; their interest rate sensitivity is apparent. However, the timing of their peaks and troughs relative to the business cycle is less than uniform, especially once a recession has begun. The first point to recognize is that permits are not a particularly good leading indicator of starts. The peaks and troughs occur roughly at the same time, often the same month. Starts have peaked before permits (two months prior, before the 1973–1975 recession) and after (four months after, before the 1981–1982 downturn). Generally, they both peak anywhere from six months to a year before a recession, with 10 to 12 months the most prevalent. From there the relationship between the housing sector and the business cycle breaks down. Housing starts and permits bottomed at the very beginning of both the 1970 and 1981–1982 recessions, two months after the onset in the first case and four months after the onset in the second case. They did not bottom until one to two months after the 1974–1975 recession ended. It is also interesting to note that starts and permits bottomed in the same month in three of the last seven recession, with starts bottoming one month before permits in three others. (See Figures 14–1a, 14–1b, 14–2a, 14–2b.)

Chapter 15

Industrial Production and Capacity Utilization

General Description

The industrial production index (IP), which is available from 1919, is one of the oldest economic statistics on the economy. Industrial production measures output in manufacturing, mining, and utility industries, and it is released by the Federal Reserve together with capacity utilization data. For the calculation of the production data, which is partly based on manufacturing hours data, the Bureau of Labor Statistics provides the Federal Reserve with the manufacturing hours data on the Wednesday before it is available to the public.[1] This practice, which expe-

Economic Indicator Information at a Glance

Market Significance	Moderate
Typical Release Time	9:15 AM Eastern Time About 15th Day of Month
Released By	Federal Reserve Board
Period Covered	Prior Month

---

1   This observation was made by Manuel Johnson, who was a former vice-chairman of the Federal Reserve Board.

FIGURE 15–1 Industrial Production Index

Measured by Market and Industry Groupings

	1992
Market Groupings	**Shares**
Total Index	100%
Total Products	59.0
Final Products	45.6
Consumer Goods	26.2
Durable	5.6
Auto & Trucks	1.6
Nondurable Goods	20.5
Total Equipment	19.4
Business Equipment	15.3
Defense and Space Equipment	3.5
Intermediate Products	13.5
Construction Supplies	5.2
Business Supplies	8.3
Total Materials	41.0
Durable Goods	21.0
Nondurable Goods	9.4
Energy	10.6
Special Market Groupings	
Total excluding autos and trucks	97.3
Total excluding motor vehicle and parts	95.3
Total excluding computer and office equipment	96.3
Industry Groupings	
Total Index	100.0
Manufacturing	84.6
Mining	7.3
Utilities	8.1
Special Industry Groupings	
Manufacturing less motor vehicle and parts	79.8
Manufacturing less computer and office equipment	80.9

dites the calculation of industrial production, has fueled speculation from time to time about when the Federal Reserve chairman knows about this information. Moreover, for internal purposes only, the Federal Reserve staff (at the chairman's request) created a weekly production index (which is far less comprehensive) for more timely updates, which are provided to the Federal Reserve Board of Governors.

Analyzing the Data

Since 1987 *industrial production* has been compiled from 255 series based on the 1987 Standard Industrial Classification (SIC) system. Industrial production is based on physical volume data for 39 percent of the index (as measured on a value-added weight basis), while the remainder of the index is based on employee hours (which accounts for another third of the index) and electricity data (as measured by kilowatt hours, accounting for about a quarter of the index). The data are divided into industry and market groupings, which are shown in Figure 15–1. Several special categories are reported, such as total less auto and trucks and total less computer equipment, since each of these industries can have a big one-month impact on the index due to a pickup in production plans. Hence, to get a feel of the broad-based underlying strength or weakness, it is useful to look at those special groupings.

The Federal Reserve also compiles a *production diffusion index*—which measures the net percentage of components rising for the 255 industries. Theory and empirical studies suggest that the production diffusion index contains information that is not found in the IP series itself.[2] Indeed, former Federal Reserve Board Chairman Arthur Burns even developed a "theory of diffusion" in his early days. But the usefulness of the production diffusion index is somewhat diminished by its one additional month reporting lag; hence, the financial markets tend to overlook this indicator (internally, the Fed computes an estimate of the diffusion index on a current-month basis).

---

2   See: Kennedy (1991).

Capacity utilization is the ratio of actual output to a trend-growth in capacity. On a monthly basis, the capacity utilization rate tells us little more than is already known directly from changes in industrial production because capacity is assumed to expand on trend. However, it does help put production changes and economic activity into a longer term context. Still, Alan Greenspan, the chairman of the Federal Reserve, correctly observed that capacity is "a somewhat elusive concept," since it is not clear whether a high rate of capacity utilization will lead to (1) higher prices, (2) higher output, or (3) a pickup in foreign goods demand. In reality, all three events occur even though the financial markets generally focus only on the price implication. Moreover, the concept of capacity assumes a fixed labor and capital input. In the short run, however, new technologies have reduced the labor input and produced an improvement in manufacturing productivity, which makes the interpretation even more tricky.

The statistical relationship between wholesale prices and capacity utilization is shaky because statistically the crude producer prices less food and energy leads changes in the capacity utilization rate when tested against a lead of 6 or 12 months. However, at the finished goods level, the PPI less food and energy follows the capacity utilization rate when tested against a timing difference of 6 months, but the reverse is true for a 12-month lead/lag relationship. This clearly suggests that one should not read too much "inflation implication" into the capacity utilization rate. Nonetheless, market participants do read inflation implication into the utilization rate; Figure 15–2 shows some rough rules.

It is important to note that in Figure 15–2 the current capacity utilization rate has a 12-month lead time with core finished goods inflation. In addition to the inflation relationship, capacity utilization is often viewed as a trigger to higher or lower capital spending. Statistically, however, capacity utilization and real capital spending move concurrently. The rules of thumb to interpret capacity utilization and spending are shown in Figure 15–3.

FIGURE 15–2 Core Producer Prices and Capacity Utilization
(Prices Lagged 12 Months, Relationship Between 1977–1992)

Capacity Utilization Rate	Implication for Inflation
86.0%	7.5%
85.0	6.9
84.0	6.4
83.0	5.8
82.5	5.5
82.0	5.2
81.5	4.9
81.0	4.7
80.5	4.4
80.0	4.1
79.5	3.8
79.0	3.5
78.5	3.2
78.0	3.0
77.0	2.4
76.0	1.8

FIGURE 15–3 Capacity Utilization and Real Capital Spending
(Concurrent, Relationship, 1967–1992)

Capacity Utilization Rate	Implication for Capital Spending
86%	16.9%
85	13.4
84	10.0
83	6.5
82	3.0
81	0
80	-3.9
79	-7.4
78	-10.9
77	-14.3

FIGURE 15–4a Industrial Production

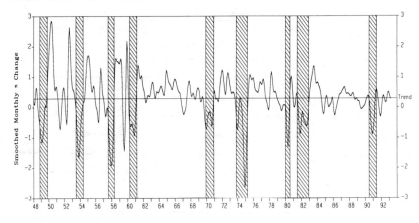

Note: Shaded areas represent business cycle recessions

FIGURE 15–4b Industrial Production
(January 1948–December 1992, Percent Change)

		Normal Bounds				Series Characteristics	
Period	Historic Low	Normal Low	Average	Normal High	Historic High	Standard Deviation	Share of Total Observations
Recession	−4.2% in Dec 1974	−1.3 %	−0.8%	−0.3 %	+2.2% in Feb 1982	1.0 pp.	96	18.1%
Recovery	−0.9% in Dec 1982	+0.5 %	+0.9%	+1.4 %	+3.5% in Mar 1950	0.9 pp.	123	23.3%
Expansion	−3.4% in Aug 1959	−0.1 %	+0.4%	+0.9 %	+6.6% in Aug 1952	1.0 pp.	310	58.6%

Industrial Production and Capacity Utilization over the Business Cycle

Industrial production follows a normal cyclical pattern with the strongest gains found in the recovery period. During recessions, industrial production declines on average by 0.8 percent per month with a normal band of -1.3 percent to -0.3 percent. During the recovery phase, production tends to increase by a hefty 0.9 percent per month and then settle down to a trend 0.4 percent pace during expansions. On the other hand, the capacity utilization rate tends to be higher during the recession than the recovery phase of the business cycle. On average, the capacity utilization rate is 80.3 percent during recessions and 78.8 percent

FIGURE 15–5a Capacity Utilization Rate

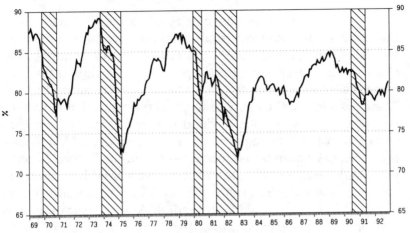

Note: Shaded areas represent business cycle recessions

FIGURE 15–5b Capacity Utilization Rate
(January 1967–December 1992, Rate)

Period	Historic Low	Normal Bounds			Historic High	Series Characteristics		
		Normal Low	Average	Normal High		Standard Deviation	Share of Total Observations	
Recession	72.6% in Nov 1982	78.4 %	80.3%	82.3 %	87.3% in Dec 1973	3.9 pp.	57	18.3%
Recovery	71.8% in Dec 1982	77.5 %	78.8%	80.2 %	84.2% in Jun 1977	2.7 pp.	83	26.6%
Expansion	78.4% in Jun 1986	82.6 %	84.0%	85.4 %	89.2% in Oct 1973	2.8 pp.	172	55.1%

during recoveries. This type of pattern occurs since the early stages of a recovery are dominated by low utilization, which improves over the course of the recovery due to the pickup in output and slowly growing or still declining capital stock. The average capacity utilization rate during expansions has been 84.0 percent with a normal high of 85.4 percent and a series high of 89.2 percent in October 1973 (which was on the verge of the 1973–1975 recession). (See Figures 15–4a, 15–4b, 15–5a, and 15–5b.)

Special Factors, Limitations, and Other Data Issues

There are numerous conceptual concerns that have been raised about the industrial production index regarding the form and factor inputs in the production function. For example, does electricity use properly reflect capital use? Or, should the electricity data be incorporated as a separate factor of production? These are some of the many conceptual problems that have been wrestled with by regional Federal Reserve Banks in their own attempts to produce regional production indexes. Other questions that have been raised include—should the Federal Reserve produce a service production index, which would be the counterpart to the industrial output series for service producing industries? In fact, for a while the Federal Reserve was doing just that on an experimental basis. Although it was more heavily dependent on hours data than would be ideal, it was a recognition of the role of services and extension industrial output methodology.

Relationship with Other Series

Because employee hours directly accounts for one-third of the industrial production index and indirectly reflects monthly business conditions, it is a standard forecasting practice to use components of the employment report to forecast industrial production. The weekly production indexes such as the *Business Week* index are far less comprehensive than the monthly series compiled by the Federal Reserve. (But the *Business Week* index moves similarly to the Federal Reserve's internal weekly index, since there are only a handful of weekly production series available.)

References

Industrial Production—1986 Edition, Board of Governors of the Federal Reserve System, Washington, D.C., 1986.

"Industrial Production Revision," *Federal Reserve Bulletin*, Vol. 79 (June 1993).

Kennedy, James, "Empirical Relationships Between the Total Industrial Production Index and Its Diffusion Indexes," *Finance and Econom-*

ics Discussion Series, Working Paper No. 163, Board of Governors of the Federal Reserve, Washington, D.C., July 1991.

Sharpio, Matthew D., "Assessing the Federal Reserve's Measures of Capacity and Utilization," *Brookings Papers on Economic Activity*, 1989, Vol. 1, pp. 181–242.

Chapter 16

Leading Economic Indicator

General Description

The composite index of leading economic indicators (LEI) is a basket of 11 cyclical indicators selected among the Commerce Department's seven major economic areas. Those economic areas encompass (1) employment and unemployment, (2) production and income, (3) consumption, trade, orders, and deliveries, (4) fixed-capital investment, (5) inventories and inventory investment, (6) prices, costs, and profits, and (7) money and credit. The LEI's purpose is to signal turning points in the economic cycle as quickly as possible.

Economic Indicator Information at a Glance

Market Significance	Low
Typical Release Time	8:30 AM Eastern Time About 23d-25th Business Day After End of Month
Released By	Commerce Department Bureau of Economic Analysis
Period Covered	Prior Month

Analyzing the Data

The U.S. Commerce Department's composite index of leading economic indicators was devised to anticipate business cycle turning points in the economy. (See Figures 16–1a and 16–1b.) The components were selected based on their breadth and reliability in forecasting turning points over history. All of the source data used in the calculation of the LEI are released in some form prior to the release of that current month's LEI, which makes estimates of the LEI relatively easy. But that does not diminish the importance of the LEI—at least at signaling turning points—since research has suggested that the composite indexes contain more information than most of the individual components of the composite indicator.[1]

The current form of the composite index of leading indicators is composed of 11 series:

1. Average weekly hours in manufacturing
2. Average weekly initial claims for unemployment insurance
3. Manufacturers' new orders for consumer goods and materials (1982 dollars)
4. Vendor performance
5. Contracts and orders for plant and equipment (1982 dollars)
6. Housing permits.
7. Change in durable goods unfilled orders (1982 dollars, smoothed)
8. Change in sensitive materials prices (smoothed)
9. Stock prices (S&P 500, monthly average)
10. Real M2
11. University of Michigan's consumer expectations index

Two companion cyclical measures exist: a coincident indicator and a lagging indicator of business-cycle turning points. The composite index of coincident indicators is composed of (1) industrial production, (2) personal income less transfer payments (1987 dollars), (3) nonagricultural employment, and (4) manufacturing and trade sales (1987 dollars). The lagging indicator includes (1) the average duration of unemployment, (2) the manufacturing and trade inventory-to-sales ratio (1987 dollars), (3) the change in labor cost per unit of output for manufacturing

---

1   See, for example, Niemira and Fredman (1991).

FIGURE 16–1a Composite Index of Leading Indicators

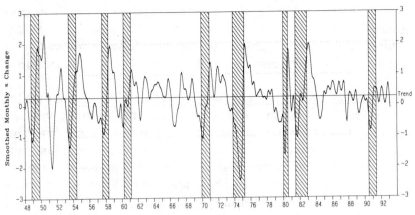

Note: Shaded areas represent business cycle recessions

FIGURE 16–1b Composite Index of Leading Indicators
(February 1948–December 1992, Percent Change)

Period	Historic Low	Normal Bounds			Historic High	Series Characteristics	
		Normal Low	Average	Normal High		Standard Deviation	Share of Total Observations
Recession	−3.4% in Mar 1980	−0.9 %	−0.3 %	+0.3 %	+3.0% in Sep 1949	1.2 pp.	96	18.1%
Recovery	−1.3% in Feb 1981	+0.6 %	+1.0 %	+1.4 %	+3.2% in Apr 1975	0.8 pp.	123	23.3%
Expansion	−2.9% in Jun 1951	−0.2 %	+0.2 %	+0.6 %	+4.0% in Jul 1950	0.8 pp.	310	58.6%

FIGURE 16–2 Composite Index of Coincident Indicators
(February 1948–December 1992, Percent Change)

Period	Historic Low	Normal Bounds			Historic High	Series Characteristics	
		Normal Low	Average	Normal High		Standard Deviation	Share of Total Observations
Recession	−4.7% in Oct 1949	−1.4 %	−0.9 %	−0.5 %	+1.7% in Sep 1949	0.9 pp.	96	18.1%
Recovery	−0.7% in Nov 1991	+0.4 %	+0.7 %	+1.1 %	+2.8% in Mar 1950	0.7 pp.	123	23.3%
Expansion	−3.5% in Jul 1956	−0.1 %	+0.4 %	+0.9 %	+8.6% in Jan 1987	1.0 pp.	310	58.6%

FIGURE 16–3 Composite Index of Lagging Indicators
(February 1948–December 1992, Percent Change)

Period	Historic Low	Normal Bounds			Historic High	Series Characteristics	
		Normal Low	Average	Normal High		Standard Deviation	Share of Total Observations
Recession	−4.4% in Jul 1980	−0.8 %	−0.2%	+0.4 %	+2.4% in Mar 1980	1.1 pp.	96	18.1%
Recovery	−3.9% in May 1958	−1.0 %	−0.4%	+0.2%	+2.8% in Dec 1980	1.1 pp.	123	23.3%
Expansion	−1.5% in Dec 1959	+0.2%	+0.6%	+1.1 %	+4.7% in Sep 1959	0.9 pp.	310	58.6%

(smoothed), (4) prime rate, (5) commercial and industrial loans (1982 dollars), (6) ratio of consumer installment credit to personal income, and (7) the change in the CPI for services (smoothed). The lagging indicator generally is viewed as a proxy for the cost pressures in the economy. (See Figures 16–2 and 16–3.)

The ratio of the coincident-to-lagging indicator composites has a longer lead time at business cycle peaks than even the leading indicator, which provides a reason to look at this aggregate. For the seven business cycles between 1957–1992, the leading indicator had an average lead of 9.3 months at business cycle peaks (with a range of two months to 20 months), while the ratio of the coincident-to-lagging indicator had an average lead of 16.3 months (with a range of nine months to 27 months).

Leading Indicator over the Business Cycle

The leading indicator composite tends to grow at a 0.2 percent pace during expansions, which is far slower than the 1.0 percent average pace that characterizes the recovery phase of the cycle. The normal fluctuation around the expansion mean for the leading indicator composite is 0.8 percentage points, which means that it is not unusual to have the leading indicator decline during an expansion. This, of course, makes interpretation difficult. During recessions, the leading indicator has declined by an average of 0.3 percent, with a normal band of 1.2 percentage points around the average.

Special Factors, Limitations, and Other Data Issues

The main goal of the leading indicator composite is as a precusor of business-cycle turning points. As such, it tends to have limited appeal at other times when the economy is recording solid growth—whether it is slow, moderate, or strong. But since the leading indicator is a sensitive measure of economic activity, it tends to dip ahead of growth-cycle slowdowns as well. It is at those times that the indicator itself can be difficult to read. Moreover, studies showed that a three-month decline rule for the leading indicator is not reliable in calling a turning point. Hence, more elaborate frameworks have been devised to distinguish growth-cycle and business-cycle turning point signals. Some of the more popular techniques used today include (1) Neftci's (Hamilton) sequential probability method and (2) Zarnowitz and Moore's sequential signals. The Neftci technique suddenly took on market significance in 1990 following a comment by Federal Reserve Board Chairman Alan Greenspan in which he cited the probability of a recession, which was based on the Neftci calculation. In addition to its use in signaling turning points in the economy, the Neftci-Hamilton method has been used in calling turning points in various markets, including the bond market (Coons 1994), the stock market (Niemira 1990), and the foreign exchange market (Engel and Hamilton 1990).

Relationship with Other Series

The cyclical indicators are a repackaging of existing economic data into a more informative fashion. They are "end products."

References

Coons, James W., "Predicting Turning Points in the Interest Rate Cycle," in Michael P. Niemira and Philip A. Klein, *Forecasting Financial and Economic Cycles,* John Wiley & Sons, New York, 1994.

Diebold, Francis X., and Glenn D. Rudebusch, "Scoring the Leading Indicators," *Journal of Business,* Vol. 62, No. 3 (1989), pp. 369–391.

Engel, Charles, and James D. Hamilton, "Long Swings in the Dollar: Are They in the Data and Do the Markets Know It?" *American Economic Review,* Vol. 80, No. 4 (September 1990), pp. 689–713.

Hamilton, James D., "A New Approach to the Economic Analysis of Nonstationary Time Series and the Business Cycle," *Econometrica,* Vol. 57, No. 2 (March 1989), pp. 357–384.

Neftci, Salih, "Optimal Prediction of Cyclical Downturns," *Journal of Economic Dynamics and Control,* 1982, pp. 225–241.

Niemira, Michael P., "Forecasting Turning Points in the Stock Market Cycle and Asset Allocation Implications," in Philip A. Klein, ed., *Analyzing Modern Business Cycles,* M.E. Sharpe, Armonk, N.Y., 1990, pp. 109–127.

Niemira, Michael P., "An International Application of Neftci's Probability Approach for Signaling Growth Recessions and Recoveries Using Turning Point Indicators," in K. Lahiri and G. Moore, eds., *Leading Economic Indicators: New Approaches and Forecasting Records*, Cambridge University Press, New York, 1991, pp. 91–108.

Niemira, Michael P., and Giela T. Fredman, "An Evaluation of the Composite Index of Leading Indicators for Signaling Turning Points in Business and Growth Cycles," *Business Economics*, October 1991, pp. 49–55.

Palash, C. J., and L. J. Radecki, "Using Monetary and Financial Variables to Predict Cyclical Downturns," *Federal Reserve Bank of New York Quarterly Review*, Summer 1985, pp. 36–45.

Stock, James H., and Mark W. Watson, "New Indexes of Coincident and Leading Economic Indicators," *NBER Macroeconomics Annual 1989*, The MIT Press, Cambridge, Mass., 1989, pp. 351–394.

Chapter 17

Manufacturing Orders, Inventories, and Shipments

General Description

This series is a more comprehensive version of the durable goods orders report. It includes orders, shipments, and unfilled orders data for the nondurable manufacturing sector and also incorporates inventory data, something not provided in the durable goods orders report. In terms of breadth, it is the best picture of the manufacturing sector offered by government statistics, covering most manufacturing companies with 1,000 employees or more. Diversified companies must file separately for divisions that operate in different industrial areas.

Economic Indicator Information at a Glance

Market Significance	Low
Typical Release Time	10:00 AM Eastern Time Six Business Days After Durable Goods Orders
Released By	Commerce Department Census Bureau
Period Covered	Two Months Prior

Orders

Orders are defined as the intent to purchase for immediate or future delivery. They must be supported by legal documents (purchase agreements, letters of intent, etc.), and they are the net nominal value between current month's orders and cancellations of previous orders. Orders also are not directly accounted for in the survey. They are derived as the sum of shipments plus the change in unfilled orders. A key reason for this is that many companies supply new orders data only for those areas with an order backlog.

Durable goods orders account for 50 percent of the total and 75 percent of the volatility. Although nondurable orders can show sharp changes, they cannot match the extremes of durable goods orders. In the period from 1980 through 1993, durable goods orders had a maximum one-month increase of 12.1 percent and a maximum drop of 10.7 percent, while nondurable orders' biggest one-month gain was 4.8 percent and their sharpest one-month drop was 4.0 percent. Specific nondurable orders, on a dollar basis, just cannot match the effect on the series of orders for big-ticket items like aircraft, machinery, or military hardware.

Manufacturing orders have a strong cyclical pattern, as one would expect. Their historic low is a drop of 6.6 percent during the 1974 recession, while the largest increase recorded was a 6.7 percent increase in 1991. Their ability to lead the cycle, particularly to the downside, is historically obscured by the mid-1970s recession. Then there was a tremendous amount of inventory speculation that resulted in manufacturing orders rising until 10 months after the recession had begun. A more reasonable picture of the series relationship with the business cycle are the 1970 and 1981/1982 recessions. Then orders peaked, on a level basis, three months before the downturn began.

Finally, it needs to be noted that the inherent nature of the orders series allows for great volatility. Orders have risen close to 5 percent during recessions and have dropped close to 4 percent during recoveries. Consistency is not the hallmark of orders.

Shipments

Sales and shipments are the same thing. They are measured by the receipts, billings, or value of product shipped.

Inventories

Inventories are determined by the book value of stocks at the end of the month. They are broken into three categories: finished goods, work in progress, and materials and supplies. Each company uses its own method of valuation.

With so much information coming out, it's difficult to ascribe any singular characteristic to the data. Each series has its own behavior pattern, and on a month-to-month basis, each shows varying degrees of volatility.

Manufacturing inventories account for approximately 45 percent of all inventories. During times of growth, the month-to-month variability is not particularly great; the normal range for both the recovery and expansion phases is only four-tenths of 1 percent for each growth phase. The breakdown into finished goods, work in progress, and materials and supplies can offer broad interest in terms of the business cycle; but on a month-to-month basis, it carries little market importance. A further discussion of this component will be grouped into the business inventories section.

Unfilled Orders

Industry backlog (unfilled orders) qualitatively work off two other series. The first is obviously new orders. The other is production capacity. At the initial stages of a recovery, spare capacity is available to meet not only existing orders, but also the new orders inflow. Thus, unfilled orders usually decline as a recovery begins. It's only when new orders rise long enough to boost production to capacity limits (generally speaking, above 83 percent for the economy as a whole) that orders will "back up." This is best illustrated by the fact that the average increase in unfilled orders is greatest during the expansion phase of a business cycle, not during the recovery. Suffice it to say that following orders matters much more than following unfilled orders.

Although it's a separate release, the business inventory series takes the inventory component of the manufacturing data directly. The GDP accounts also utilize the manufacturing inventory data, although it is well massaged and not the only measure that the Bureau of Economic Analysis employs for gauging inventory accumulation. The BEA also takes a shipments component, nondefense capital goods ex aircraft, as an indicator of business spending on equipment.

Analyzing the Data

Given all of the data, one might think that the markets would show a fair amount of interest in this release. They don't. If there is a focus, it is on orders, but the fact that durable orders have already been released about a week earlier dramatically lessens the importance of the orders series. Nondurable orders typically do not show enough volatility to change the picture already provided by the durable component. Under the circumstances one watches for any revision to the durable component and then gets a handle on the nondurable change. However, it's information for information's sake.

From there, a case can be made for looking at inventories but only for an underlying view of the economy—not in terms of immediate market impact. One can spin a general picture for the economy—inventories being run down or run up, leading to production increases or cuts—but for the markets that potential result has to be apparent in other key series, such as industrial production, orders, and retail sales, before the story is worth trading upon. This point of reference is even more pertinent to the unfilled orders data, while the shipments data is basically a nonevent. In short, analysis of the manufacturing orders, inventories, shipments, and unfilled orders release is brief and of very modest market value, although analysts can get a lot out of the report.

Manufacturing Orders over the Cycle

Manufacturing orders are a leading indicator of the business cycle; they peak before recessions begin and bottom out before the recovery takes off. The average rate of growth, however, follows the business cycle very closely. Manufacturing orders average a 0.4 percent drop in recessions but then show a rather robust average gain of 1.2 percent in recoveries. Growth is still apparent in the expansion phase of the business cycle but at a slower +0.6 percent pace. Unfilled orders, being a lagging indicator, show their strongest gains in the expansion phase. This is when capacity constraints have been reached and backlogs grow. (See Figures 17–1a, 17–1b, 17–2, and 17–3.)

FIGURE 17–1a Factory Orders

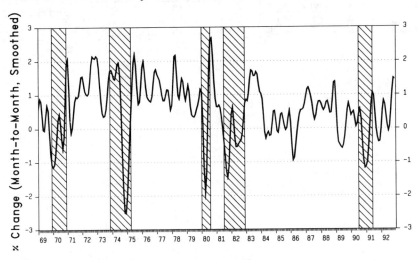

Note: Shaded areas represent business cycle recessions

FIGURE 17–1b Factory Orders
(March 1958–December 1992, Percent Change)

| Period | Historic Low | Normal Bounds | | | Historic High | Series Characteristics | |
		Normal Low	Average	Normal High		Standard Deviation	Share of Total Observations
Recession	−6.6% in Dec 1974	−1.6 %	−0.4%	+0.8 %	+4.7% in Jan 1974	2.4 pp.	69	16.5%
Recovery	−3.7% in Dec 1991	+0.2 %	+1.2%	+2.3%	+6.7% in July 1991	2.1 pp.	104	24.9%
Expansion	−4.6% in Jan 1978	−0.4 %	+0.6%	+1.6%	+6.6% in Dec 1988	2.0 pp.	245	58.6%

FIGURE 17–2 Factory Unfilled Orders
(February 1958–December 1992, Percent Change)

| Period | Historic Low | Normal Bounds | | | Historic High | Series Characteristics | |
		Normal Low	Average	Normal High		Standard Deviation	Share of Total Observations
Recession	−2.9% in Feb 1958	−0.8 %	−0.2%	+0.4%	+3.1% in Aug 1974	1.2 pp.	70	16.7%
Recovery	−1.3% in Apr 1975	−0.1 %	+0.3%	+0.8%	+2.7% in Mar 1959	0.9 pp.	104	24.8%
Expansion	−2.6% in Jan 1960	+0.3%	+0.8%	+1.3%	+3.4% in Mar 1973	1.0 pp.	245	58.5%

FIGURE 17–3 Factory Inventories

(February 1958–December 1992, Percent Change)

Period	Historic Low	Normal Bounds			Historic High	Series Characteristics		
		Normal Low	Average	Normal High		Standard Deviation	Share of Total Observations	
Recession	−1.2% in Dec 1960	−0.3 %	+0.7%	+1.7%	+13.9% in Jan 1982	1.9 pp.	70	16.7%
Recovery	−1.2% in Jan 1983	−0.1 %	+0.2%	+0.5%	+1.2% in Jun 1976	0.5 pp.	104	24.8%
Expansion	−1.0% in Jan 1986	+0.3%	+0.5%	+0.8%	+1.6% in Jun 1979	0.5 pp.	245	58.5%

Chapter 18

Merchandise Trade

General Description

The merchandise trade report details the monthly exports and imports of goods of the United States. Service flows are not included. The data is released in a seasonally adjusted format on a nominal and real basis and is broken down into categories more detailed than the markets would ever care to know; hair and waste materials and nuclear fuel materials exports and imports have never been known to move markets.

Economic Indicator Information at a Glance

Market Significance	Varies: Moderate-to-High
Typical Release Time	8:30 AM Eastern Time Third Week of the Month
Released By	Commerce Department Census Bureau
Period Covered	Two Months Prior

The importance of the trade data to the financial markets has varied over the years. In the mid- to late 1980s, the release was the most important, even surpassing the employment report. Then, the U.S. dollar was the most important financial variable, and any information that had implications for the dollar's direction became critically important. But as the greenback's wild swings became a thing of the past, the markets lost interest in the trade report. Now, the merchandise trade report is of moderate interest to financial markets.

The Commerce Department groups the trade flows into six major end-use categories: foods and feeds, industrial supplies, capital goods ex automotive, automotive vehicles and parts, consumer goods ex autos, and other merchandise. It is these categories that are the basis of analysis once a trade number has been released. (See Figure 18–1.)

The trade balances with all major trading partners and various regions is also detailed on a nonseasonally adjusted basis. Its highly unusual for individual trade balances to have a significant effect on financial markets, although the trade balance with Japan has taken on political overtones. Japan's surplus with the United States accounted for one-third of our deficit in 1992. The resulting frictions and trade negotiations between the two countries are likely to make this particular trade balance an ongoing political issue. But as far as trading responses to the data, even this politically charged number is of only minor importance. (See Figure 18–2.)

Two other interesting ways of analyzing the trade data are to break out the ex petroleum deficit and the ex autos deficit. The deficit on petroleum accounts typically accounts for one-half of our total trade deficit; the other half (approximately) is accounted for by our deficit "ex autos." (See Figure 18–3.)

FIGURE 18–1 Shares of Trade: 1992

	Exports	Imports
Foods and Feeds	8.4%	5.4%
Industrial Supplies	26.0	26.9
Capital Goods		
Ex Autos	39.5	24.8
Autos and Parts	9.5	17.4
Consumer Goods		
Ex Autos	10.9	21.8
Other Merchandise	5.6	3.3

FIGURE 18–2 Shares of Trade for Selected Countries and Geographic Areas: 1992

	Exports	Imports
Canada	20.5%	18.8%
Western Europe	28.2	21.0
U.K.	5.3	3.8
Germany	5.1	5.4
Japan	11.5	18.7
Mexico	7.8	6.4
OPEC	4.4	6.8
NICs	10.8	12.1
Other Developing	9.4	9.1

FIGURE 18–3 U.S. Trade Deficit: Three Views

($ billions)

	1990	1991	1992
Total Deficit	-101.718	-65.399	-67.773
Ex Petroleum	-47.205	-21.781	-30.720
Ex Autos	-51.800	-20.503	-30.804

Quarterly Balance of Payments Trade Data

There are two other reports issued by the Commerce Department covering international flows. One is the balance of payments trade data, released in the second month of the quarter and covering the previous quarter. It essentially is a reworking of the monthly merchandise trade data, with the differences primarily definitional, such as the exact monthly timing of trade flows and the definition of gold and other categories. It also includes only goods. The most comprehensive picture of our international flows, and one that includes services and income, is the current account data. It is issued in the middle of the final month of the quarter for the previous quarter. The balance of payments trade data go directly into the current account series, and both are inputs in the computation of GDP, as always with the necessary BEA adjustments.

Analyzing the Data

For the foreign exchange markets, the overall balance is usually the key statistic. And when the U.S. dollar is of paramount policy importance, that would be the case for domestic financial markets as well. But under most circumstances, once the domestic markets are apprised of the overall deficit, the first order of business is to determine what happened to exports. Exports have a direct bearing on the rate of growth in the economy; therefore, they have a greater importance for the financial markets than do imports. The latter offer an implicit reflection of demand for goods within the United States. Beyond that, their interpretive relevance is somewhat obscure. Import growth may reflect inventory building, something that could portend slower growth rather than the superficial implication of faster growth. This ambiguity typically relegates the import sector to the "back burner" when the number is first released.

The next order of business is to discern whether particular export or import categories have had an overwhelming effect on the month's change. In general, there are few specific export or import components that are capable by themselves of significantly affecting the trade balance. Two that can are petroleum products on the import side and aircraft on the export side of the ledger. Petroleum products' effect on the deficit is greatest when the price of oil is moving sharply. Aircraft exports are the single largest export category, which accounts for a portion of their ability to impact the month trade data, but just as important is the fact that shipments of aircraft (for obvious reasons) can be very lumpy and distort a given month's export figure.

Market reactions to trade data can be very complicated. The weighted relevance of the export change versus the overall trade balance change depends tremendously upon whether or not U.S. policy makers are making the U.S. dollar a primary focus. For example, a rising deficit composed partially of falling exports could push fixed-income markets in either direction. If the greenback is an issue, the fact that the deficit rose and exports fell would strongly infer that the dollar needs to fall to help lower the deficit. The inflationary implications of such a presumed fall would be negative for fixed-income participants. But if the U.S. dollar and inflation are not a prime matter of concern, the singular fact that exports fell could push fixed-income prices higher and equity prices lower, since superficially such a drop would infer slower economic growth.

Merchandise Trade over the Business Cycle

Unlike other economic sectors, there is no consistent relationship between the trade balance and phases of the business cycle. During recessions net exports have run the gamut from deteriorating to showing little change to outright improvement. Clearly, a major reason is the different timing of business cycles here and abroad over time, as well as the extent of the business cycle changes here and abroad. Even imports on a level basis have not shown a clear relationship to the business cycle. The biggest factor accounting for this has been the secular deterioration of the United States' international deficit highlighted by the country's secularly rising demand for imported goods. From 1960 to 1990, on a real basis, imports as a percentage of gross domestic product have risen from 4.9 percent to 11.5 percent, a trend that can obscure what would otherwise be obvious changes in our import demand. Exports have shown consistent growth during the expansionary phase of our business cycles, but the relationship again goes awry during recessions and recoveries. (See Figures 18–4a and 18–4b.)

International Price Indexes

The international price program conducted by the BLS provides monthly price indexes for U.S. imports and exports. Respondents are asked to provide prices that include all discounts, allowances, and rebates. Export price indexes are measured on a f.a.s. (free alongside ship) basis; import price indexes are measured both on a f.a.s. basis and on a f.o.b. basis (free on board), which allows the BLS to measure the shipment cost to the export destination. The international price indexes have fixed weights, which currently are set from shares of 1985 value of imports and exports as compiled by the Bureau of the Census. These data are used to deflate the monthly merchandise trade statistics.

FIGURE 18–4a Merchandise Trade Balance

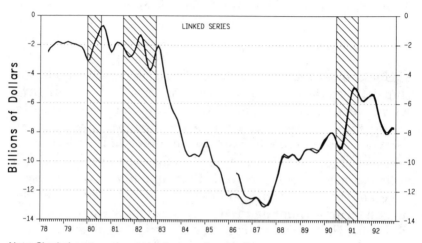

Note: Shaded areas represent business cycle recessions

FIGURE 18–4b Merchandise Trade Deficit
(January 1978–December 1992, Level, Billions of Dollars)

Period	Historic Low	Normal Bounds			Historic High	Series Characteristics	
		Normal Low	Average	Normal High		Standard Deviation	Share of Total Observations
Recession	−$9.5 bn. in Nov 1990	−$5.3 bn.	−$3.9 bn.	−$2.5 bn.	+$0.2 bn. in Apr 1982	$2.8 bn.	30	16.7%
Recovery	−$9.3 bn. in Apr 1984	−$6.4 bn.	−$5.0 bn.	−$3.7 bn.	+$0.4 bn. in Mar 1981	$2.7 bn.	42	23.3%
Expansion	−$14.1 bn. in Oct 1987	−$10.0 bn.	−$8.1 bn.	−$6.1 bn.	−$0.2 bn. in Jan 1978	$3.9 bn.	108	60.0%

Chapter 19

NAPM Purchasing Managers' Index

General Description

The National Association of Purchasing Management (NAPM) survey was created out of a necessity to monitor the economy and ultimately the economy's impact on the pricing environment. In its early days, the NAPM survey provided information on national business trends that was unavailable elsewhere.

Economic Indicator Information at a Glance

Market Significance	High
Typical Release Time	10:00 AM Eastern Time First Business Day of the Month
Released By	National Association of Purchasing Management
Period Covered	Prior Month

However, since the initial days of the survey, government data sources exist and provide more comprehensive and quantifiable measures for many of the concepts that are surveyed by NAPM. NAPM began to formally survey its membership to gauge business conditions in 1931. Today, the survey committee consists of over 300 persons selected from a cross-section of 20 manufacturing industries to reflect each industry's contribution to the gross national product. The trade association draws its survey participants primarily from a membership list of 34,000 persons.

The purchasing executive is asked in the questionnaire (see Figure 19–1) to evaluate the change in his/her firm's

- Employment,
- Prices,
- Supplier,
- Delivery time,
- Production,
- Inventories,
- Lead times of purchased items,
- New orders from customers,
- New export and import orders, and
- Order backlogs (a new component introduced in 1993 at Federal Reserve Board Chairman Greenspan's suggestion.)[1]

The survey participant's formal responses to the questions are limited to an evaluation of *higher, lower,* or *unchanged* compared to the prior month, yet the respondent also is encouraged to add voluntary comments. Each component of the survey is compiled into a *diffusion index* following the convention of adding the percentage of the sample rising (or falling) plus one-half of the percentage of the sample responding "same" or "no change." The diffusion index can range between 0 and 100 percent, and it measures the breadth or strength of change, with 50 percent implying no net change; above 50 percent suggesting improvement; and below 50 percent representing a contraction. A summary measure of business activity is formulated as a composite diffusion index, which is called the *Purchasing Managers' Index* (PMI),[2] based on a weighted average of new orders, production, employment, supplier delivery time, and inventories. The PMI summary measure is assigned the following weighting scheme:

$$PMI = 0.30 \times (New\ Orders) + 0.25 \times (Production) + 0.20 \times (Employment)$$
$$+\ 0.15 \times (Supplier\ Deliveries) + 0.10 \times (Inventories)$$

---

1   The survey questions continually have evolved. The new export orders question was introduced in January 1988 and an import orders question began in October 1989.

2   This index, which was originally called the NAPM composite diffusion index, was formulated under the direction of Theodore Torda, who is a senior economist at the U.S. Department of Commerce.

FIGURE 19–1 Business Survey Questionnaire

REPORT FOR NAPM BUSINESS SURVEY COMMITTEE

Answers should reflect the responsibility level of YOUR purchasing organization (plant, division, company) and essentially only for the SIC that you have indicated in the available space. It is essential that questions only have ONE answer, that ALL questions are answered, and that completed forms are returned or faxed no later than the date indicated. You are encouraged to consult others in your company in order to provide current and accurate answers to all the questions.

1. GENERAL REMARKS: Comment regarding any business condition, local, national, or international, that affects your purchasing operation or the outlook for your company or industry. Your opinion and comments are very important.
Remarks: _____

2. PRODUCTION—Check the ONE box that best expresses the current month's level compared to the previous month.
 ❑ Better than a month ago   ❑ Same as a month ago
 ❑ Worse than a month ago
Remarks: _____

3. NEW ORDERS—Check the ONE box that best expresses the current month's new orders compared to the previous month.
 ❑ Better than a month ago   ❑ Same as a month ago
 ❑ Worse than a month ago
Remarks: _____

4. NEW EXPORT ORDERS—Check the ONE box that best expresses the current month's new export orders compared to the previous month.
 ❑ Do not Export   ❑ Better than a month ago
 ❑ Same as a month ago   ❑ Worse than a month ago
Remarks: _____

5. ORDER BACKLOGS—Check the ONE box that best expresses the current month's order backlog compared to the previous month.
 ❑ Same as a month ago   ❑ Higher than a month ago
 ❑ Lower than a month ago
Remarks: _____

6. COMMODITY PRICES—Check the ONE box that best expresses the current month's change in approximate net-weighted average prices of the commodities you buy compared to the previous month.
- ❏ Higher than a month ago   ❏ Same as a month ago
- ❏ Lower than a month ago

List, in the spaces provided, specific commodities (use generic names, not proprietary) which are up or down in price since the last report. This may or may not involve announced price changes.

Up in price: _____

Down in price: _____

7. INVENTORIES OF PURCHASED MATERIALS—Check the OVERALL inventory level (units, not dollars) including raw, MRO, intermediates, etc. (not finished goods unless purchased) compared to the previous month.
- ❏ Higher than a month ago   ❏ Same as a month ago
- ❏ Lower than a month ago

Reasons if higher or lower: _____

8. IMPORTS—Check the ONE box that best expresses the current month's overall imports (units, not dollars), including raw, MRO, components, intermediates, etc. (not finished goods unless purchased) compared to the previous month.
- ❏ Do not Import   ❏ Higher than a month ago
- ❏ Same as a month ago   ❏ Lower than a month ago

Remarks: _____

9. EMPLOYMENT—Check the OVERALL level of employment compared to the previous month.
- ❏ Greater than a month ago   ❏ Same as a month ago
- ❏ Less than a month ago

Reasons if greater or less: _____

10. VENDOR DELIVERIES—Check the ONE box that best expresses the current month's OVERALL delivery performance compared to the previous month.
- ❏ Faster than a month ago   ❏ Same as a month ago
- ❏ Slower than a month ago

Reasons if faster or slower: _____

---

11. ITEMS IN SHORT SUPPLY—Report specific commodities (use generic names, not proprietary) you purchase that are in short supply, even if mentioned in previous reports.

---

12. BUYING POLICY—Indicate, by checking the ONE appropriate box for each category of purchases, the approximate weighted number of days ahead for which you are committed. Do not report hedging or speculative purchases.

Production Materials

Hand to Mouth	30 Days	60 Days	90 Days	6 Months	Year+
O	O	O	O	O	O

MRO Supplies

Hand to Mouth	30 Days	60 Days	90 Days	6 Months	Year+
O	O	O	O	O	O

Capital Expenditures

Hand to Mouth	30 Days	60 Days	90 Days	6 Months	Year+
O	O	O	O	O	O

The formal results of the survey with commentary are published in the NAPM Report on Business issued monthly by the trade association. In May and December, NAPM issues a semi-annual outlook survey, which addresses some longer term issues. (See Figure 19-2a.)

The NAPM PMI generally is reported at 10:00 a.m. (Eastern Time) on the first business day of the month for the preceding month. This makes this indicator one of the earliest measures available for the prior month, hence, it has become a key focus for the financial markets. It also provides information that is not found in any other government statistic, such as data on supplier delivery times, items in short supply, and buying policy, which is the average number of days in advance that a company has made commitments to buy (1) production materials; (2) maintenance, repair, and operating (MRO) supplies; and (3) capital expenditures. Typically, faster supplier delivery times are associated with slower business conditions, and vice versa.

FIGURE 19–2a NAPM Purchasing Managers' Index

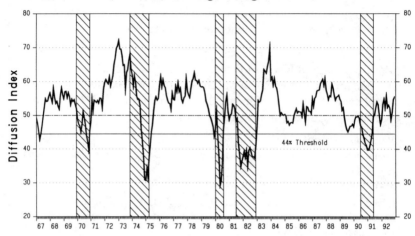

Note: Shaded areas represent business cycle recessions

FIGURE 19–2b NAPM Purchasing Managers' Index
(January 1948–December 1992, Level)

		Normal Bounds				Series Characteristics	
Period	Historic Low	Normal Low	Average	Normal High	Historic High	Standard Deviation	Share of Total Observations
Recession	29.2% in May 1980	38.7%	42.4 %	46.1%	63.6% in Dec 1973	7.4 pp.	96	18.1%
Recovery	37.5% in Apr 1975	52.7%	56.0 %	59.3%	74.7% in May 1950	6.6 pp.	123	23.3%
Expansion	36.7% in Apr 1952	52.0 %	55.3 %	58.7 %	77.5% in Jul 1950	6.7 pp.	310	58.6%

PMI over the Business Cycle

Figure 19–2b shows how the NAPM PMI behaves in different phases of the business cycle. During expansions the PMI averages 55.3 percent, while during recessions it tends to be 13 percentage points lower. During recovery phase of the business cycle, the PMI tends to be indistinguishable from the expansion readings.

Analyzing the Data

The analysis of these data should be done on five levels: (1) business-cycle turning point implications, (2) the overall implication for economic growth, (3) what the price measures imply for inflation, (4) the theme of the components, and (5) the relationship between components of the report and other government indicators.

1. Tracking the NAPM PMI as a Turning Point Indicator: There are several critical threshold levels of the PMI that have significant implication for the economy. The key threshold levels in the PMI are (1) the cyclical high, (2) 50 percent, (3) 44 percent, and (4) the cyclical low.

History suggests that the NAPM PMI is a reliable forecasting indicator of a *growth-cycle turning point.* Over the last 40 years, the NAPM PMI led growth-cycle peaks by seven months, on average, and led growth-cycle lows by three months. Hence, this leads to the following observation that the NAPM PMI cyclical "high" and "low" values have led peaks and troughs in the growth cycle. But growth-cycle, or mini-cycle, peaks and troughs do not always lead to an absolute decline or rebound in the economy.

A reading of 50 percent or less is the second threshold level to watch for in tracking manufacturing activity. By definition, the 50 percent threshold is the point at which an equal percentage of the respondents to the survey say business conditions are better as they are worse. As such, the 50 percent point is significant for the financial markets from a psychological standpoint, as well as a signal of potentially more weakness to come. On average, the PMI has fallen below 50 percent two months before recessions have begun (with a range of 14-month lead time in 1990 to a 10-month lag in 1973). When the PMI falls below 44 percent, that often signals an absolute decline in economic activity, which historically has occurred two months after the turning point date on average (see Figures 19-3a and 19-3b). It is important to recognize that this index measures only manufacturing activity; hence, the PMI must fall below 44 percent in order for it to signal a widespread contraction in the economy. This is largely because service sector industries tend to be less cyclical and/or lag manufacturing activity, which could hold up the economy even if the manufacturing sector is deteriorating.

During a recession, the PMI generally has continued to decline until it reached 34.8 percent on average (lowest 29.4 percent in 1980 and highest 43.6 percent in 1961). Once the PMI turned around, it has taken an average of four months to cross above 44 percent, which generally has occurred simultaneously

FIGURE 19–3a Tracking the NAPM Purchasing Managers' Index Over the Business Cycle Recession

Business Cycle Peak	"The High" --- Phase 1 ---			"50% Threshold" --- Phase 2 ---			"44% Threshold" --- Phase 3 ---		
	Date	Value	Timing	Date	Value	Timing	Date	Value	Timing
194811	194806	53.0	−5	194807	48.4	−4	194809	42.1	−2
195307	195208	60.4	−11	195305	48.9	−2	195308	43.5	+1
195708	195505	69.5	−27	195703	47.5	−5	195704	43.1	−4
196004	195905	68.2	−11	196003	47.8	−1	196005	42.6	+1
196912	196811	58.1	−13	197001	48.7	+1	197010	42.4	+10
197311	197301	72.1	−10	197409	46.2	+10	197410	42.7	+11
198001	197807	62.7	−18	197908	49.9	−5	197912	43.8	−1
198107	198104	53.3	−3	198107	48.3	0	198109	41.8	+2
199007	198712	61.0	−31	198905	45.4	−14	199010	43.3	+3
Average		62.0	−14.3		47.9	−2.2		42.8	+2.3

Note: Timing is measured in months from business cycle turning point dates; a minus sign implies a lead, a plus sign implies a lag.

FIGURE 19–3b Tracking the NAPM Purchasing Managers' Index Over the Business Cycle Recovery

Business Cycle Trough	"The Low" --- Phase 1 ---			"44% Threshold" --- Phase 2 ---			"50% Threshold" --- Phase 3 ---		
	Date	Value	Timing	Date	Value	Timing	Date	Value	Timing
194910	194902	31.3	−8	194908	47.0	−2	194909	52.3	−1
195405	195312	35.6	−5	195403	44.7	−2	195405	50.1	0
195804	195801	33.4	−3	195805	46.6	+1	195806	51.4	+2
196102	196102	43.6	0	196103	49.1	+1	196104	57.6	+2
197011	197011	39.7	0	197012	45.4	+1	197102	54.8	+3
197503	197501	30.7	−2	197506	45.1	+3	197508	51.4	+5
198007	198005	29.4	−2	198008	45.9	+1	198010	54.0	+3
198211	198111	34.7	−12	198301	46.0	+2	198302	54.4	+3
199103	199102	39.7	−1	199105	44.7	+2	199107	50.1	+4
Average		35.3	−3.7		46.1	+0.8		52.9	+2.3

Note: Timing is measured in months from business cycle turning point dates; a minus sign implies a lead, a plus sign implies a lag.

with a business cycle low. Finally, the PMI has never declined below 44 percent without signaling a growth or business cycle. However, from these data alone it is very difficult to distinguish between the two types of national cycles.

2. Using the NAPM PMI to Predict Real GDP and Industrial Production: The relationship with industrial production and the

NAPM PMI has become closer over time, though its lead time is rather short. On average, the PMI leads year-over-year changes in industrial production by two months. The estimated relationship between industrial production growth on a year-over-year basis (IP) and the PMI lagged two months is shown below for various periods. In the 1980–1992 period, the PMI explained nearly 74 percent of the fluctuation in industrial production.

$$IP = 0.51 \times PMI\,[-2] - 23.4 \quad R^2 = 0.7445 \quad \textit{Sample Period: } 1980\text{–}1992$$

This relationship, which has been stable over time, suggests that the PMI must exceed 45.9 percent to be consistent with flat industrial production growth. Alternatively, when the PMI is at 50 percent, that has been consistent with 2.1 percent growth in production (that is, [.51x50]–23.4). Figure 19–4a shows the near-term implication for industrial production based on the PMI.

FIGURE 19–4a Near-Term Relationship Between Production and the NAPM PMI

PMI Reading	Industrial Production Implication
60.0%	+6.9%
55.0	+4.4
50.0	+1.9
46.8	0.0
45.0	-0.6
40.0	-3.1

Although it may be conceptually risky to associate the PMI with real GDP since GDP covers services and structures in addition to goods output, the fact is that the PMI anticipates real GDP growth (year-over-year) reasonably well with a lead time of one quarter

$$GDP = 0.317 \times PMI\,[-1] - 13.9 \quad R^2 = 0.7918 \quad \textit{Sample Period: } 1980\text{–}1992$$

The estimated quarterly GDP/PMI relationship suggests a PMI reading of 43.8 percent has been consistent with no change in real GDP. Additionally, a 50 percent PMI reading has been consistent with 1.9 percent real GDP growth. Other combinations of the PMI and the real GDP year-over-year growth rate, which are derived from the equation estimated between 1980 and 1992, are shown in Figure 19–4b. The key limitation of using the PMI to

FIGURE 19–4b Near-Term Relationship Between Real GDP and the NAPM PMI

PMI Reading	Real GDP Implication
60.0%	+5.1%
55.0	+3.5
50.0	+2.0
45.0	+0.4
43.8	0.0
40.0	-1.2

forecast some of the broader macroeconomic indicators is the short lead time. Nonetheless, the PMI provides an excellent guide to what is currently happening.

Although the PMI offers limited insight into longer-term growth prospects, it is still possible to use it to forecast beyond the near term. However, as is true of every forecast, the longer the forecast horizon, the more uncertainty is associated with it. With this caveat in mind, the PMI could be used to project year-ahead growth using the following annual relationships:

$$IP = 0.521 \times (YEAREND\ [-1] - NAPM\ [-1]) + 2.4$$
$$\qquad (5.656) \qquad\qquad\qquad\qquad\qquad (4.78)$$

$$R^2 = 0.7111 \quad Sample\ Period:\ 1978–1992,\ Annual$$

where *IP* is annual industrial production growth, *YEAREND* is the December NAPM PMI index for the prior year, and *NAPM* is the annual average PMI, also for the prior year. The numbers in parentheses are t-statistics for the coefficients. The use of the December level of the NAPM PMI minus its annual average serves as a momentum indicator; that is, if the year ends higher than the annual average, that suggests the positive momentum will continue, and vice versa. Similarly, an estimated equation also can be derived for real GDP, which is as follows:

$$GDP = 0.329 \times (YEAREND)\ [-1] - NAPM\ [-1]) + 2.34$$
$$\qquad (4.865) \qquad\qquad\qquad\qquad\qquad (6.209)$$

$$R^2 = 0.6635 \quad Sample\ Period:\ 1978–1991,\ Annual$$

where, *GDP* is annual real GDP growth. These two equations allow for a longer-term view.

3. Prices Diffusion Index—A Leading Indicator of Inflation:
The NAPM business survey committee is asked each month to
average the prices that they paid for goods and services and to
indicate whether prices rose, fell, or stayed the same compared
to the prior month. A number of studies have shown that the
diffusion index compiled from this question is a leading indicator of turning points in the inflation cycle.[3] However, it does not
provide a reliable indication of one-month changes in the producer price index. Nonetheless, one study showed that the price
diffusion index explained 59 percent of the fluctuation in one-
month-ahead estimates of changes in the producer price index
for intermediate materials and supplies.[4]

**4. The Unfolding of the Business Cycle Through the NAPM
Business Survey:** The NAPM survey provides a relatively complete picture of manufacturing activity. Hence, at different
stages of the business cycle, different measures are worth dwell-
ing upon. For example, coming out of a recession, one would
expect that the new orders diffusion index would perk up first,
followed by production. Supplier lead times would tend to
lengthen, suggesting that business activity is firming as well—
though the greater adherence to just-in-time (JIT) inventories
and the closer partnership of suppliers and customers is likely
to limit the cyclical information from this measure in the future.
As the economy continues to improve, employment and inventories should notch higher. With a lag, prices will begin to reflect
the strengthening economy. Similarly, the NAPM survey can be
used to watch the unfolding of a slowdown or recession. New
orders would be an early indicator to reflect weakness in the
economy, which tends to spread to supplier delivery times, production, and prices. Generally, the economic weakness will
show up in the employment and inventories diffusion indexes
last.

5. Other Links with Government Data: There are government data series that conceptually match components of the

---

3   See, for example, Howard Roth, "Leading Indicators of Inflation," *Economic
     Review*, Federal Reserve Bank of Kansas City, November 1986, pp.3-20. Also see:
     Michael Niemira, "Updated PW Leading Indicator of Inflation," Paine Webber,
     December 26, 1986.
4   Lahiri and Dasgupta (1990).

NAPM survey. For example, the NAPM employment diffusion index is conceptually similar to the U.S. Bureau of Labor Statistics' (BLS) manufacturing employment diffusion index. However, the government series tends to be more comprehensive, and the two measures can often move in different directions in the very near term. The NAPM price diffusion index is similar to the commodity price diffusion indexes calculated by the Commerce Department, and the NAPM production diffusion index is conceptually similar to the Federal Reserve's industrial production diffusion index calculated over one-month intervals. The Federal Reserve series also is more comprehensive than the NAPM measure, but it is reported with a one-month lag, which makes the NAPM series more timely.

Finally, one very near-term barometer of future business conditions that is sometimes calculated from the purchasing manager survey detail is the difference of the new orders and inventories indexes, which conceptually is similar to a ratio of a leading indicator to a lagging indicator. The Purchasing Management Association of Oregon (PMAO), for example, presents such a monthly index with their monthly survey, which has been dubbed their monthly *forecasting index*. Statistically, the correlation between the PMI and the difference between the national measures of new orders and inventories is highest with a one-month lead time, which means that the same methodology used by PMAO can be applied to the national data. Based on this methodology, a simple one-month-ahead forecasting relationship can be derived as follows:

$$PMI = 0.831 \times PMI[-1] + 0.386 \times FCINDEX[-1] - 12.36$$

$$R^2 = 0.8793 \quad \textit{Sample Period}: 1980\text{--}1990$$

where *FCINDEX* is the forecast index, which is expressed in a similar fashion as the PMI and is calculated as (New Orders minus Inventories) divided by 2 plus 50.

Special Factors, Limitations, and Other Data Issues

These data have been developed primarily to monitor the manufacturing sector. Hence, the *Report on Business* measures activity in about 22 percent of the U.S. economy (measured as a share of real GDP). Moreover, these data are qualitative and not quantitative. The survey has been criticized for a sampling bias, its "backward-looking" nature, and its subjective responses.[5] But these findings view the survey simply as a means to an end, instead of as a separate and reasonably reliable barometer of manufacturing activity. Clearly, these survey data provide an easy way to track the economy without too much data intensity. Furthermore, research suggests that the breadth of a recovery, expansion, or recession contains information on future growth prospects, which is another reason to monitor diffusion indexes.[6]

Columbia University Center for International Business Cycle Research (CIBCR), with a grant from the NAPM, has reformulated the NAPM information into a *leading index*, which they argue is conceptually more accurate and cyclically more reliable. This, in part, follows from the view that some measures of the PMI are conceptually not leading indicators such as employment and production. The CIBCR index consists of four components from the monthly survey; namely, new orders, supplier deliveries, prices, and inventories, and it is adjusted for the long-term trend in the economy.

In addition to the national survey, numerous regional purchasing manager associations around the country survey local

---

5   Harris (1991). Harris concluded that his "results suggest that the index is flawed ... it is a poor leading indicator and on its own it can be a misleading measure of short-run movements in the economy." (p.13) One valid criticism of the construction of the summary measure that has been put forth by Klein and Moore (1988) is that the inventory component should enter the composite index as a change, not as a level. The parallel for this argument is how inventories are treated within the national income accounts. Gross domestic product (GDP) is the sum of final demand plus the *change* in inventories (which is the concept measured by the NAPM survey question. As for the timing concern that Harris raises between, say, the NAPM PMI and industrial production, one way to statistically address this issue is to test for what is known as "Granger causality" between the two measures. A simple application of this test between 1980 and 1991 with one, three, and six lags suggests that there is strong evidence that the NAPM PMI "Granger-causes" changes in industrial production. Essentially, this means that the Harris criticism is overstated.

6   Kennedy (1991). This idea that diffusion or the breadth of change is important for the unfolding of the business cycle is not new. Arthur Burns (the former Federal Reserve Chairman) and William Fellner (a former member of the President's Council of Economic Advisors) were both advocates of that hypothesis. The Fellner hypothesis, which is known as the Law of Diminishing Offsets, argued that business cycle recessions occurred as a result of prior diminution of dispersion of growth rates.

purchasing manager executives. Probably the best known of the regional surveys is the Chicago survey. Purchasing Management Association (PMA) of Chicago generally releases their local area business conditions report on the last business day of the month at 10:00 (Eastern time) for that same month. Consequently, the Chicago survey often is viewed as a window on the more comprehensive NAPM report. The typical question that financial market participants ask once the Chicago survey is released is: "what does the regional survey results mean for the NAPM report?" In evaluating the Chicago survey for its national implication, it is important to keep in mind the following: (1) the Chicago Business Barometer (CBB), which is the summary measure released with the Chicago report, is compiled differently from the NAPM PMI. The CBB includes order backlogs (unfilled orders), while the NAPM index does not; the CBB does not include inventories, but the NAPM index does. (2) The weighting scheme also is different (see Figure 19–5). The new orders component has a larger weight in the CBB than it does in the NAPM PMI, while the CBB employment component has half the importance as in the NAPM index. Both measures are seasonally adjusted, but the Chicago index is seasonally adjusted at the total level while the NAPM index is seasonally adjusted by component and summed.

Some other regional and industry purchasing manager surveys often are released prior to the national survey, which focuses attention on those surveys as well. The Detroit, Buffalo, Milwaukee, and the *Electronic Buyers' News* (EBN) QUEST reports tend to be released before the national report.

To find out more about these regional purchasing manager surveys, a list of those currently available is provided below. But

FIGURE 19–5 A Comparison Between the CBB and the NAPM PMI

(What Is Included and the Associated Weight)

	Production	New Orders	Employment	Deliveries	Inventories	Backlogs
CBB	0.25	0.35	0.10	0.15	Not Included	0.15
NAPM PMI	0.25	0.30	0.20	0.15	0.10	Not Included

new surveys continually are being implemented by regional purchasing managers' groups.

Besides the regional purchasing association surveys, an electronic industry purchasing manager survey is conducted by *Electronic Buyers' News* and is published monthly in their publication. The EBN index, which has been dubbed *QUEST*, is compiled identically to the national survey.[7] The Federal Reserve Bank of Philadelphia conducts a monthly survey of local manu-

Regional Purchasing Manager Surveys		
Location	**Sponsor**	**Phone**
Arizona	PMA of Arizona	(602) 752-7890
Austin, TX	PMA of Austin	(512) 345-0552
Boston, MA	NAPM–Boston	(508) 371-2522
Buffalo, NY	PMA of Buffalo	(716) 731-6263
Chicago, IL	PMA of Chicago	(312) 782-1940
Cincinnati, OH	NAPM–Cincinnati	(513) 731-2222
Cleveland, OH	PMA of Cleveland	(216) 391-8300
Detroit, MI	NAPM–Metro Detroit	(313) 222-4000
Grand Rapids, MI	Grand Rapids Association of Purchasing Management	(616) 323-1531
Mid-America	Drake University	(515) 271-2001
Milwaukee, WI	PMA of Milwaukee	(414) 786-1880
New York, NY	NAPM–New York	(718) 739-4900
Oregon	PMA of Oregon	(503) 725-3728
Rochester, NY	PMA of Rochester	(716) 726-7713
Rock River Valley, IL	PMA of Rock River Valley	(815) 962-8841
South Bend, IN	PMA of South Bend	(616) 683-0437
Southwestern, MI	NAPM–Southwestern Michigan	(616) 323-1531
Toledo, OH	NAPM–Toledo Area	(419) 537-2430

---

7   The EBN name is a holdover from when the survey was quarterly. The term *QUEST* was derived from *Quarterly Electronics State-of-the-Industry* report.

facturers, which is called the *Business Outlook Survey* (BOS), and it is very similar to the purchasing managers' surveys. The BOS also asks local manufacturers to provide a six-month ahead forecast of various business barometers, such as capital spending, prices, employment, and so forth. In late 1991, the Federal Reserve Bank of Atlanta began a monthly survey of Southeast manufacturing conditions, which is structured similarly to the Philadelphia FRB survey. Unfortunately, there is little consistency between most of the purchasing managers' regional surveys and even the national survey, which is conducted totally independently of the regional associations and does not incorporate any survey input from the regional association surveys. Regional surveys are summarized in *Electronic Buyers' News* and in NAPM *Insights,* which is the official publication of NAPM. In evaluating the regional surveys, it is important to note whether or not the data is seasonally adjusted (most regional surveys do not seasonally adjust their data) and be aware whether the survey is solely manufacturing based or whether it includes respondents from nonmanufacturing firms (e.g., the Boston survey includes service establishments). There is nothing wrong with including nonmanufacturing firms in the survey, but for cross-country comparisons that distinction must be clear to the user. Because regional coverage and methodologies may differ widely across surveys, most regional surveys are more appropriate for historical comparisons within the region and may not be appropriate for geographic comparisons. Another practical concern with the regional surveys is that due to the generally smaller sample size than the national, the regional surveys can be more choppy, even if the data are put on a consistent basis. Finally, some regional surveys prefer to report their results as net difference indexes or net percentage rising (NPR). The NPR is simply the percentage of respondents reporting higher minus the percentage reporting lower. The net difference, which is bounded by +100 and 100, is related to the diffusion index as follows:

$$NPR = 2 \times (DI - 50)$$

where DI is the diffusion index. Similarly, the identity can be reformulated as

$$DI = 50 + \left(\frac{NPR}{2} \right)$$

The choice of which formula to use for expressing the direction of survey change is arbitrary.

References

Ammer, Dean S., "The N.A.P.M. Business Survey: How it Works. How To Use It as a Purchasing Tool," National Association of Purchasing Management, 1983.

Bretz, Robert J. "Behind the Economic Indicators of the NAPM Report on Business," *Business Economics*, July 1990, pp. 42–47.

Bretz, Robert J., "Forecasting with the *Report on Business*," NAPM *Insights*, August 1990, pp. 22–25.

Harris, Ethan S., "Tracking the Economy with the Purchasing Managers, Index," Research Paper No. 9124, Federal Reserve Bank of New York, August 1991.

Hoagland, John H., and Barbara E. Taylor, "Purchasing Business Surveys: Uses and Improvements," *Freedom of Choice: Presentations from the 72nd Annual International Purchasing Conference*, National Association of Purchasing Management, 1987.

Kennedy, James E., "Empirical Relationships Between the Total Industrial Production Index and Its Diffusion Indexes," Finance and Economics Discussion Series 163, Board of Governors of the Federal Reserve System, Divisions of Research and Statistics and Monetary Affairs, July 1991.

Klein, Philip A., and Geoffrey H. Moore, "N.A.P.M. Business Survey Data: Their Value as Leading Indicators," *Journal of Purchasing and Materials Management*, Winter 1988, pp. 32–40.

Lahiri, Kajal, and Susmita Dasgupta, "A Comparative Study of Alternative Methods of Quantifying Qualitative Survey Responses Using NAPM Data," Working Paper, State University of New York at Albany, August 14, 1990.

"Purchasing Managers, Commerce Department Develop New Economic Index," U.S. Department of Commerce News, Office of Economic Affairs, February 4, 1982 (which was simultaneously issued as a NAPM press release).

Torda, Theodore, "Purchasing Management Index Provides Early Clue on Turning Points," *Business America*, Vol. 8, pp. 11–13.

Chapter 20

Personal Income and Consumption

General Description

Personal consumption expenditures (PCE) measure the value of goods and services purchased by the consumer while personal income measures all sources of income to the household sector on a cash disbursement basis. These data are the monthly counterparts to the quarterly measures, which are part of the GDP report.

Economic Indicator Information at a Glance

Market Significance	Moderate
Typical Release Time	10:00 AM Eastern Time About 21st-22nd Business Day After End of Month
Released By	Commerce Department Bureau of Economic Analysis
Period Covered	Prior Month

Analyzing the Data

Personal consumption accounts for about two-thirds of real GDP. PCE (1) measures purchases of new goods and services by business and government and in only one case measures the purchases *from individuals*, which is for household workers, services; (2) includes the purchase of goods and services of nonprofit institutions (which accounts for about 4 percent of real GDP); (3) includes the net purchases of used goods by individuals and nonprofit institutions from business and government; (4) includes the purchase of goods and services abroad by U.S. residents; and (5) also includes imputed spending on (a) housing and institutional structures and equipment that are rented or owned, (b) farm products consumed on farms, (c) wages and salaries paid in kind, and (d) some services that are furnished without payment. PCE does not include payments to governments that are a result of administrative or regulatory functions. Those are included under personal taxes and nontaxes. Personal consumption data on a monthly basis are determined by the Census Bureau's retail sales data (retail sales less auto dealers and building materials), unit car and truck sales, and extrapolation of detailed components that are available only annually. In 1992, consumer spending on services (household, medical, education, electricity and public utilities, transportation, brokerage fees, legal services, etc.) accounted for nearly 60 percent of total consumer spending. As might be expected, service spending (partly due to the high degree of extrapolation) is the least volatile component of PCE, while durable goods spending is the most volatile. Between 1959 and 1992, the average absolute deviation of the month-to-month percentage change in consumer services was 0.28 percentage points; it was 0.61 percentage points for nondurable spending, and a hefty 2.24 percentage points for durable goods spending.

Personal outlays are a slightly broader concept than personal consumption, since it includes interest paid by the consumer to business (mortgage and consumer installment interest payments—but not principal) and personal transfer payments to the rest of the world. This measure of spending is used to calculate the savings rate, which is defined as disposable personal income (personal income less taxes) minus personal outlays and divided by disposable income.

Personal income accounted for 85 percent of nominal GDP in 1992. Nearly 60 percent of personal income is made up from wages and salaries. But some relatively small components can be volatile from month to month. Farm income, which accounted for 1.1 percent of personal income in 1992, can be a very volatile component due to the lumpiness of farm subsidy payments. It is not surprising to see the farm income component jump or decline by $20 bn. (at an annual rate) in any given month, which would contribute or subtract 0.4 percentage points from the overall change in personal income for a given month. The farm subsidy program is continually changing; but as a guide, several times a year large subsidy payments are made by the U.S. Department of Agriculture. For example, December is often the time to watch for large wheat payments to farmers; in February, cotton and rice payments are often made; and in March/April, watch for corn and grain payments and advances paid to farmers.

Another source of volatility comes from the Commerce Department's imposition of bonus payments in certain months, which shows up in the wage and salary component of income. Generally, the only industry that the Commerce Department had been adjusting the income data for bonus payments was the motor vehicle industry, which paid a bonus as part of their wage agreement with their labor unions (although other industries had similar lump-sum payments that were not directly accounted). However, in December 1992 the Commerce Department broke with their tradition and adjusted personal income for the earlier than normal payment of bonuses within the securities industry. This adjustment was necessary because the Commerce Department said that their personal income estimating procedures did not account for this large bonus payment. But this adjustment raised a more far-reaching question about the methodology used by the Bureau of Economic Analysis (BEA) and the seemingly *ad hoc* nature of adjustments that are imposed from time to time.

Personal income is also adjusted for major storm or disaster loss. The adjustment is normally done through the rental income component. When the BEA identifies a major disaster impact, they adjust rental income downward by the uninsured loss amount. Nonfarm proprietors' income is also likely to be adjusted downward to reflect unisured losses to business property. But to the extent that there is insurance, personal consumption is adjusted downward. The BEA will lower property insurance services because this component of PCE is defined as the insurance premiums minus benefits. Although this adjustment will depress nominal consumption, real consumption—which is only based on premiums paid—will be unaffected, which will create an abnormal divergence between the real and nominal measures.

The market importance of the monthly personal-consumption data tends to change over a given quarter. After the advance GDP report is released, the monthly consumption data tends to have the least market significance. But over the subsequent two months, the data takes on more market importance, since it provides a timely estimate of the current quarter's real PCE and GDP pace. Personal income *less special factors*—which is a measure discussed in the Commerce Department press release but not shown in any data table—tends to have more market importance than the overall measure of personal income because it provides a better picture of the underlying income stream. (See Figure 20–1.)

Personal Consumption and Income over the Business Cycle

On a month-to-month basis, changes in personal consumption are difficult to interpret. However, on a smoothed growth-rate basis the dynamic and relationship with personal income becomes clearer. Although it is widely accepted in economic theory that consumption is dependent on income, the second part of the theoretical framework is often overlooked, which is that consumption determines income as well. This consumption-income link is considerably more important at cyclical (both major and minor cycle) turning points. *Moreover, statistical causality tests support the view that consumption leads income at cyclical turning points.*[1] Hence, the often used argument that the consumer cannot spend without income growth picking up is wrong from a cyclical perspective. Consumers often supplement their income by charging purchases, which provides the extra boost to sales needed to turn the economy around. Moreover, measures of consumer spending power, such as the savings rate, can be quite misleading in the short term for assessing the con-

---

1   Applying the Granger causality test to a three-month moving year/year growth
     rate between consumption and income lends strong support to the view that
     consumption "Granger-causes" income growth.

FIGURE 20–1 Personal Income and Consumption and
Their Components (Billions of Dollars)

		1992	
	Personal Consumption	$4,095.8	
	Durable Goods	480.4	← 11.7% of PCE
	Nondurable Goods	1,290.7	← 31.5% of PCE
	Services	2,324.7	← 56.8% of PCE
plus	Interest Paid by Persons	112.1	← 2.7% of Outlays
plus	Personal Transfer Payments to Rest of World (Net)	10.3	
equals	**Personal Outlays**	4,218.2	
		1992	
	Personal Income	5,058.1	
	Wage and Salaries	2,918.1	← 57.7% of Income
	Other Labor Income	305.7	
	Proprietors'Income	404.5	
	Farm	55.4	
	Nonfarm	376.4	
	Rental Income	4.7	
	Personal Dividend Income	139.3	
	Personal Interest Income	670.2	
	Transfer Payments	866.1	
	OASDHI Insurance	414.1	
	Government Unem-ployment	40.2	
	Other	411.8	
minus	Personal Contributions for Social Insurance	250.6	
		1992	
	Personal Income	$5,058.1	
minus	Personal Tax and Nontax Payments	627.3	
equals	**Disposable Personal Income**	4,430.8	
minus	Personal Outlays	4,218.8	
equals	**Personal Savings**	212.6	← Residual
divide	by Disposable Personal Income		
equals	Personal Savings Rate	4.8%	

sumers' spending ability, since big-ticket items leased or purchased on credit are paid off over a period of time, which does
not concurrently drain savings in the period of consumption as
might be implied by the national income methodolgy.

Personal consumption tends to grow at a 0.7 percent pace
during expansions—which is identical to its pace during the
recovery phase of the cycle. This is also true for personal income, which tends to grow at a 0.7 percent pace during the
recovery and expansion phases of the cycle. However, there is a
subtle but important difference during recessions. During recessions, consumption tends to outpace income growth by 0.1 percentage point, on average. This is significant and more of a timing difference with income than anything else. The savings rate
tends to be highest during recessions and progressively notches
lower in recovery and expansion phases of the cycle. The rise in

FIGURE 20–2a Personal Consumption

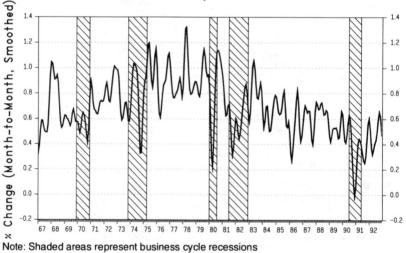

Note: Shaded areas represent business cycle recessions

FIGURE 20–2b Personal Consumption
(February 1959–December 1992, Percent Change)

| Period | Historic Low | Normal Bounds | | | Historic High | Series Characteristics | |
		Normal Low	Average	Normal High		Standard Deviation	Share of Total Observations
Recession	−1.9% in May 1960	+0.2%	+0.5%	+0.8%	+1.7% in Aug 1974	0.6 pp.	67	16.5%
Recovery	−1.0% in Feb 1984	+0.5%	+0.7%	+1.0%	+2.4% in May 1975	0.5 pp.	95	23.3%
Expansion	−1.8% in Jan 1987	+0.4%	+0.7%	+1.0%	+2.5% in Sep 1986	0.6 pp.	245	60.2%

FIGURE 20–3a Personal Income

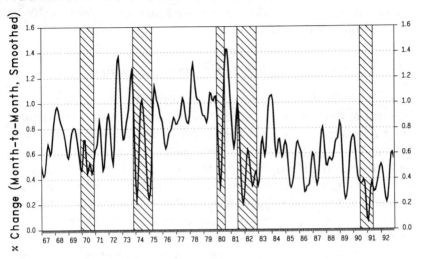

Note: Shaded areas represent business cycle recessions

FIGURE 20–3b Personal Income
(February 1959–December 1992, Percent Change)

Period	Historic Low	Normal Bounds			Historic High	Series Characteristics		
		Normal Low	Average	Normal High		Standard Deviation	Share of Total Observations	
Recession	−0.9% in Jan 1991	+0.2%	+0.4%	+0.7%	+2.3% in Apr 1970	0.5 pp.	67	16.5%
Recovery	−1.0% in Jul 1971	+0.5%	+0.7%	+1.0%	+2.6% in Jun 1975	0.5 pp.	95	23.3%
Expansion	−0.7% in Aug 1959	+0.5%	+0.7%	+1.0%	+2.7% in Sep 1965	0.5 pp.	245	60.2%

FIGURE 20–4 Personal Savings Rate
(January 1959–December 1992, Percent)

Period	Historic Low	Normal Bounds			Historic High	Series Characteristics		
		Normal Low	Average	Normal High		Standard Deviation	Share of Total Observations	
Recession	3.7% in Sep 1990	6.8%	7.6%	8.5%	10.8% in Dec 1973	1.7 pp.	67	16.5%
Recovery	0.0% in Jan 1959	6.2%	7.0%	7.8%	10.5% in May 1975	1.6 pp.	95	23.3%
Expansion	3.1% in May 1987	5.7%	6.4%	7.1%	10.5% in May 1975	1.4 pp.	245	60.2%

the savings rate during recessions reflects pent-up consumer demand, which is unleashed in better times. (See Figures 20–2a, 20–2b, 20–3a, 20–3b, 20–4.)

Special Factors, Limitations, and Other Data Issues

One of the key conceptual limitations of the personal consumption data is the treatment of consumer durable purchases as if they were fully paid for in the period in which they were purchased. Although a car can be paid off over several years, it is assumed to be bought and paid for all at the same time. As a result, the savings rate could look abnormally depressed if car and truck sales soar. Indeed, only about 8 percent of cars and light trucks are fully paid off at purchase time, while the remainder are leased or financed by conventional means. The flow-of-funds accounts, however, adjust for this and consequently develop a higher savings rate (see section on GDP).

Relationship with Other Series

The monthly measure of personal income is calculated on a "cash" or "when paid" basis, while the quarterly measure is calculated on an "accrual" or "when earned" basis. This results in accounting differences between the wage and salary components in the personal income report and the GDP report. That NIA adjustment, which is called "wage accruals less disbursements," was a relatively small $1.5 bn. in 1992.

Reference

Niemira, Michael P., "Using Composite Leading Indicators to Forecast Sales and to Signal Turning Points in the Stock Market," in K. Lahiri and G. Moore, eds., *Leading Economic Indicators: New Approaches and Forecasting Records*, Cambridge University Press, New York, 1991, pp. 355–372.

Chapter 21

Producer Price Index

General Description

The producer price index (PPI) is a fixed-weight price index that measures the average domestic change in prices, less any discounts, received by producers of commodities at the wholesale level. Imported goods prices are not directly measured in the PPI. However, to the extent they enter into a producer's costs, they can affect what producers charge and receive for their goods. The PPI covers all three stages of processing: crude, intermediate, and finished goods.

Economic Indicator Information at a Glance

Market Significance	High
Typical Release Time	8:30 AM Eastern Time About the 10th Business Day of the Month
Released By	Labor Department Bureau of Labor Statistics
Period Covered	Prior Month

The finished goods category covers products that will undergo no further processing. They will be bought and used as is. Machinery, clothing, and household items are representative of the category. Intermediate goods need additional processing. Good examples are cardboard boxes, milled steel products, plywood, and leather. Crude goods are the initial inputs, having undergone no processing. Basic commodities, such as crude oil, cotton, and iron ore, are typical of crude good components.

The data is also grouped by commodity. In this format, the specific price change reported for a specific commodity can be very misleading. If a price increase or decrease at the crude level results in price increases at the succeeding two levels, the price change for the commodity will reflect, additively, the full price change at each level. For this reason, looking at PPI commodity-based inflation changes can misrepresent the inflation picture.

The PPI surveys about 3,100 commodities via approximately 40,000 survey participants. The data are collected for the Tuesday of the week that includes the thirteenth of the month.

Unlike the Consumer Price Index, which is not subject to monthly revisions, all PPI data are subject to revision four months after the original publication. Participation in the PPI survey is voluntary, and sometimes not enough data for a particular component is available for first calculation. Subsequent, comprehensive price information can then result in revisions to the producer price index. Similar to the Consumer Price Index, annual seasonal factor adjustments are incorporated each February.

Several PPI components are used to deflate the GDP data, particularly the inventory component. Chief among them are the industrial commodities component and farm and petroleum products.

One of the key points about the PPI and one of the basic differences between the PPI and the CPI is that the producer price index is solely a commodity-based index. For now, there is no accounting for service sector inflation in the PPI. However, that is in the process of changing. The BLS has created a price index for hospital services, and it is in the midst of an ongoing operation to include that and other service sectors in the PPI. As of early 1992, the hospital services index still was not part of the PPI; it was being published as a separate index, but the inclusion of the service sector in the future appears well on its way.

Given that the PPI does not include services, the first division of the PPI is into the energy sector, food sector, and all other, or the core sector. All three stages of processing (crude, intermediate, and finished) goods are broken down into these three components. (See Figure 21–1.)

An aspect of the PPI worth noting is its greater volatility compared to the CPI. One reason is the greater relative importance of the very erratic food and energy sectors in the PPI; they ac-

FIGURE 21–1 PPI Finished Goods: Relative Importance: 1992*

Food, Energy and Core Sectors	
Food	22.4%
Energy	13.9
Core	63.7

*For an understanding of relative importances, please see the section on page 166.

count for approximately 36 percent of the PPI versus 23 percen in the CPI. But even the core, or ex food and energy, PPI is more volatile than the core CPI. First, the further down the processing chain, the more fully will an initial price shock show through. (The same analysis applies to the crude, intermediate, and finished goods levels within the PPI.) Second, we come back to the point that the PPI does not include services. As discussed in the CPI section, service sector inflation is less volatile than goods sector inflation. For these reasons, the potential to see an outright month-to-month decline in the PPI is many times greater than for the CPI. (See Figure 21–2.)

In terms of breaking the PPI down into key categories, the wholesale inflation measure is not as amenable to such an exercise as the CPI. The most basic division is into consumer goods

FIGURE 21–2 PPI: Annual Rates of Inflation: 1985–1992
December-over-December Percentage Change

Food, Energy and Core								
	1985	1986	1987	1988	1989	1990	1991	1992
Core	2.4%	2.3%	2.4%	3.3%	4.4%	3.7%	3.5%	2.4%
Food	-0.7	2.6	2.1	2.8	5.4	4.7	-0.2	-0.7
Energy	-4.0	-27.9	-2.0	-3.2	9.8	13.9	4.4	-0.4

Agricultural Prices

One of the aids for forecasting the part of the producer price index is the Department of Agriculture's agricultural price series. It's released at 3:00 p.m., usually on the last business day of the month that the data covers. The data is broken into prices paid by farmers and prices received by farmers, with the latter being the series that is often utilized to help forecast the food component of the PPI and the CPI. The data include inter alia, livestock and product prices, dairy products, and fresh fruits and vegetables, and is offered on a nonseasonally adjusted basis only for the total of all prices received. There are seasonally adjusted breakdowns for components such as fresh fruits and vegetables, dairy products, and poultry. The series' volatility greatly exceeds the food component of either of the two price indices. And, in fact, its relationship is not particularly tight with either food component. Although it is not the norm, it certainly isn't unusual for agricultural prices to decline (increase) while the two food components rise. In the latter half of 1990, agrcultural prices fell seven months in a row. The unadjusted food component of the PPI fell only three times in that period, and the CPI's component did not drop once.

---

and capital equipment. The relative importance of each is 76.9 percent and 23.1 percent, respectively. From there, however, there are no such groupings as apparel or transportation as there are in the Consumer Price Index. One is forced to immediately jump to individual price components for information on the sources of any unusual inflation news.

Analyzing the Data

One appraises the producer price index essentially as one does the CPI. Focus is placed immediately upon the month-to-month change in the overall PPI and the core PPI with the core rate change as important, if not more so, than the overall PPI. Annual inflation rates are not important at the time of release. A disparity between the overall gain and the core rate is the first thing to note, again due to the aberrant nature of change in the energy and food sectors. A much different than expected PPI

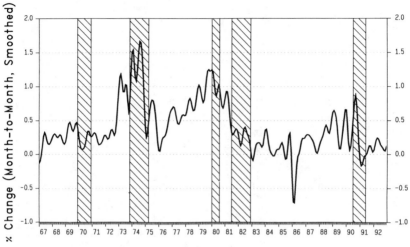

FIGURE 21–3a Producer Price Index—Finished Goods

Note: Shaded areas represent business cycle recessions

FIGURE 21–3b Producer Price Index—Finished Goods
(January 1948–December 1992, Percent Change)

Period	Historic Low	Normal Bounds Normal Low	Average	Normal High	Historic High	Standard Deviation	Share of Total Observations
Recession	−1.1% in Feb 1949	0.0 %	0.3 %	0.7 %	+2.7% in Jul 1974	0.7 pp.	96	18.1%
Recovery	−0.8% in Jan 1983	0.0 %	0.2 %	0.4 %	+1.2% in Mar 1981	0.4 pp.	123	23.3%
Expansion	−1.3% in Feb 1986	0.1 %	0.3 %	0.6 %	+3.5% in Aug 1973	0.5 pp.	310	58.6%

change that is matched with an expected core rate change is much less likely to affect the markets than is an expected PPI change coupled with a core rate change that is far from expectations. A reading two-tenths or greater from expectations would be considered a surprise, and more than likely generate a market reaction.

Once the two rates have been assimilated, the data is broken down. As already mentioned, there are no convenient, broad-based categories as in the CPI. One immediately must begin rummaging through a list of approximately 54 nonfood, nonenergy components, such as tobacco, passenger cars, women's apparel, household appliances, and pharmaceutical

FIGURE 21–4a Producer Price Index Less Food and Energy

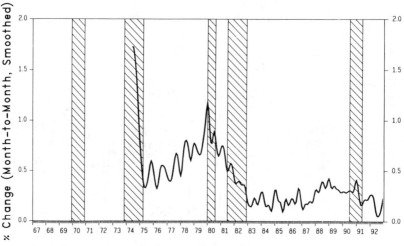

Note: Shaded areas represent business cycle recessions

FIGURE 21–4b Producer Price Index Less Food and Energy
(February 1974–December 1992, Percent Change)

		Normal Bounds				Series Characteristics	
Period	Historic Low	Normal Low	Average	Normal High	Historic High	Standard Deviation	Share of Total Observations
Recession	0.0% in Feb 1982	0.5 %	0.7 %	1.0 %	+2.2% in May 1974	0.5 pp.	44	19.4%
Recovery	−0.4% in Jan 1983	0.3 %	0.4 %	0.6 %	+1.1% in Jan 1981	0.3 pp.	69	30.4%
Expansion	−0.6% in Sep 1985	0.3 %	0.4 %	0.6 %	+2.0% in Jan 1980	0.3 pp.	114	50.2%

preps to discover the source of any unexpected price change. Again, the focus is to determine whether or not one or two components can be isolated as the source of the surprise, or whether or not it is a more broad-based change, one that may signal a change not only in one month's inflation rate, but also in the trend inflation rate as well.

Again, as with the CPI, the financial markets can become accustomed to recurring inflationary pressures emanating from specific sectors and more readily dismiss them. The tobacco and car components are the two most indentifiable at this point in time, but others could conceivably fill the bill in future years. The theme of this willingness to ignore specific price pressures is consistent with the markets' desire to focus on the underlying inflationary picture, not transitory phenomenon.

Producer Prices over the Cycle

The cyclical attributes of the PPI can be analyzed in two ways: in terms of its own relationship to the business cycle and in terms of its cyclical relationship to the CPI. Producer prices' peaks and troughs (based on annual rates of inflation) assymmetrically lag the business cycle. The peaks typically are reached within three to six months of the top of economic activity. The troughs, however, typically lag the bottom of the business cycle by about nine months. In terms of the CPI, the timing relationship between the two price indices is closely linked. More often than not, peaks and troughs for the PPI and the CPI have occurred in the same quarter and almost certainly within one quarter. For all of these relationships, there are of course exceptions, but that does not change the general thrust of observation—that inflation lags the business cycle, and the PPI and CPI have similar cyclical patterns. (See Figures 21–3a, 21–3b, 21–4a, and 21–4b.)

Measuring Price Change: What Is a Relative Importance?

The BLS's consumer and producer price indexes are constructed as a "weighted average of relatives," which means that the index shares are derived from the price of a specific commodity or service divided by the total value of purchases. The BLS publishes "relative importances" for December of the prior year, and these commonly—but incorrectly—are referred to as "weights." Relative importances actually change every month and really are *price-adjusted quantity weights.*

It is possible to keep the relative importances up-to-date by adjusting them for the latest change in price. Current relative importances are derived by dividing the December index into the equivalent current period price index, then multiplying the result by a published December relative importance. After this is done for each series making up a total, these relative importances are summed and divided by its equivalent broader aggregate relative importance for December. This results in a growth rate in the price for the total series. In turn, this is multiplied by the December total index, which yields the current index.

In practice, thankfully, it is not necessary to update relative importances during the years since the last published relative importance is generally close enough to approximate the contribution of any given component. However, when a price (such as energy prices) moves sharply higher or lower *during* a given year, that is the time to be careful about using the published relative importance. An example of this is when a huge price increase of aircraft during 1992 cut its relative importance within the PPI (the relative importance moves in the opposite direction of the relative change in the price). The relative importance of aircraft dropped to 1.912 in December 1992 from 4.118 in December 1991. Again, thankfully, this degree of change tends to be the exception rather than the rule.

Chapter 22

Retail Sales

Description of the Series

The retail sales report, issued by the Bureau of the Census, is the first but not the most comprehensive picture of consumer spending for a given month. (The personal consumption expenditures data is a more exhaustive treatment; its inclusion of all services is the key reason).

Economic Indicator Information at a Glance

Market Significance	High
Typical Release Time	8:30 AM Eastern Time Mid Month
Released By	Commerce Department Census Bureau
Period Covered	Prior Month

The estimated value of total retail sales is determined by the source of the sale, the establishment, and not by the end user. Thus, regardless of the end user (i.e., a manufacturer or even a wholesale operation), a sale made by these establishments is considered a retail sale. On the other hand, a retail sale made by a wholesaler is not part of the retail sales series. For definitional purposes, a retail establishment is defined as "a business that sells goods primarily for individual or household use."

The data include cash or credit sales, with discounts and refunds excluded. Excise taxes are included if paid by the manufacturer or wholesaler and passed onto the consumer, but they are excluded if paid directly by the purchaser and remitted to local, state, or federal authorities. This pertains to sales taxes as well.

It's not possible to say the number of retail establishments that are surveyed. A company's employer identification number is used for classification purposes, and some businesses will use one such number for the entire organization while others will use a separate number for each individual location within the selling enterprise.

In estimating retail sales volume, the Bureau of the Census breaks its universe into a sample of big companies, and three samples of smaller business establishments. The big companies report every month. Each of the three small business samples report once a quarter. Thus, the advance estimate of retail sales (the first estimate for a month) consists of reports from big companies and one small business sample. The next month a second small business sample reports for both the current month and the previous month. By the final report (the third month), all of the reporting establishments have supplied sales figures. This reporting method certainly accounts for a part of the variability and volatility in the retail sales series. But just as important is that when the Bureau of Census requests data from the establishments, within the first week of the subsequent month, many still do not have hard figures for sales, especially smaller businesses.

Retail sales data are used for GDP calculations. The Bureau of Economic Analysis takes the sales of all retail establishments ex building materials, hardware, and garden supplies, mobile homes, and motor vehicle dealers.

The retail sales report is broken down by type of product sold. The first cut is durable and nondurable. Within the durable sector, which accounts for approximately 35 percent of the total estimated retail sales volume, there are three major components reported; namely, building materials, automotive dealers (which cover cars and trucks), and furniture, home furnishing, and appliance stores. These three categories account for over 80 percent of durable purchases. (The remaining 20 percent, accounted for by inter alia, sporting goods shops, and book and jewelry stores, is not broken out in the report.) The nondurable sector is dominated by the food store category, which represents approximately 20 percent of retail sales, with general merchandise stores (department, variety, etc.) the next largest contributor. There are also detailed estimates provided for gasoline stations, apparel stores, eating and drinking establishments, liquor stores, and drug and proprietary stores. (See Figure 22–1.)

FIGURE 22–1 Retail Sales Contribution by Major Type of Establishment: 1992*

Durable Goods	36%
Building Materials	5%
Auto Dealers	20%
Furniture Dealers, etc.	5%
Other	6%
Nondurable Goods	64%
General Merchandise Stores	12%
Food Stores	20%
Gasoline Stations	7%
Apparel Stores	5%
Eating and Drinking Establishments	10%
Drug and Proprietary	4%
Liquor Stores	1%
Other	5%

*Total will not add to 100. Categories present in retail sales report do not represent the total aggregate.

There is one other key breakdown for retail sales, and it's in keeping with the recurring habit of analyzing data series without a particular component. In this instance, it is automobile dealer sales that are "ex'ed" out. This component, retail sales ex autos, is reported right alongside the change in retail sales. As is the case with other series that are reported with specific components removed, the logic is that the volatility of those specific series overstates the swings in the underlying series. An additional reason is that there is another picture of auto purchases already available; namely, unit car sales (see Chapter 3). In fact, the unit sales data are much more reliable and the Bureau of Economic Analysis uses the unit car sales data to develop its estimate of GDP growth—not the retail sales estimate of automobile sales.

Analyzing the Data

Much like the CPI and the PPI, the key "ex" component carries as much, if not more, weight as the change in the overall series. In fact, to the extent unit auto sales for the month in question are already known, it is the ex auto component that really is the only new news. This is especially so because the unit auto data are a more reliable representation of auto purchases. (They, not the retail sales component, are the basis for GDP estimates of consumer automobile expenditures.) In a sense the ex auto component is used to verify or refute what car sales are already known to have done; they fill out the consumer spending picture for the month. Thus, in a retail sales report in which the total change and the ex auto change are at opposite ends of the spectrum, something which is not unusual, it is the ex auto component that would typically determine the market's response.

Once the two major readings are understood, attention is turned to the various components. Keys to the strength or weakness of the report are based on which components account for the change. As is the case with all statistics, the more broad-based the change, the more meaningful it is. Also, it is important to differentiate between those components that can be categorized as discretionary-spending categories and nondiscretionary. Typically, the former is accounted for by the durable components and on the nondurable side of the ledger, general merchandise store sales and apparel store sales. If the spending (or lack thereof) is concentrated in these areas, then the report will have to be considered that much stronger (or weaker). Food and gasoline sales are typically considered nondiscretionary-spending categories. If the report is affected excessively by these two categories, the analysis and interpretation of

FIGURE 22–2a Retail Sales

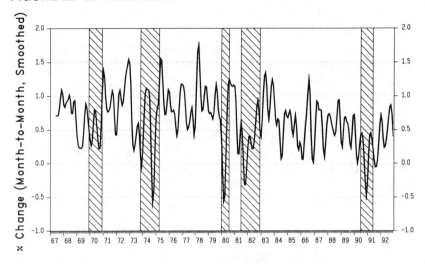

Note: Shaded areas represent business cycle recessions

FIGURE 22–2b Retail Sales
(February 1967–December 1992, Percent Change)

Period	Historic Low	Normal Bounds			Historic High	Series Characteristics	
		Normal Low	Average	Normal High		Standard Deviation	Share of Total Observations
Recession	−2.6% in Dec 1973	−0.4 %	+0.3%	+1.0 %	+3.7% in Jan 1975	1.4 pp.	57	18.3%
Recovery	−1.5% in Aug 1983	+0.3 %	+0.8%	+1.4 %	+4.6% in May 1975	1.1 pp.	83	26.7%
Expansion	−6.5% in Jan 1987	0.0 %	+0.7%	+1.4 %	+5.9% in Sep 1986	1.4 pp.	171	55.0%

FIGURE 22–3 Retail Sales Less Auto Dealers
(February 1967–December 1992, Percent Change)

Period	Historic Low	Normal Bounds			Historic High	Series Characteristics	
		Normal Low	Average	Normal High		Standard Deviation	Share of Total Observations
Recession	−1.6% in Dec 1974	0.0 %	+0.4%	+0.9 %	+3.1% in Jan 1975	0.9 pp.	57	18.3%
Recovery	−1.7% in Feb 1976	+0.2 %	+0.6%	+1.1 %	+4.1% in May 1975	0.9 pp.	83	26.7%
Expansion	−2.1% in Jan 1968	+0.3 %	+0.7%	+1.2 %	+3.7% in Sep 1967	0.9 pp.	171	55.0%

the data can change significantly. This evaluation takes the "ex-ing" out process one step further (and to some one step too far), but the logic is that in an effort to gauge consumer-spending psychology, purchases of essentials is not a useful tool. In regard to the food and gasoline components, the fact that price changes can cause much of the sector volatility is an added reason to play down their contribution to the final retail sales result. Thus, a 1 percent increase in retail sales ex autos, which contains a 2 percent increase in food store sales and a 1.5 percent increase in gasoline sales, would not be construed as being nearly as negative for the bond market and positive for equity markets as a similar gain that was concentrated in furniture, general merchandise, and apparel purchases.

One final analytical point is the importance of revisions to retail sales, more so than many other series. They can be substantial; thus, their impact can potentially supersede or totally offset the current month's reading. Revisions of 1 percent are not uncommon to both total retail sales changes and the ex auto component, and they can carry back two months.

Retail Sales over the Cycle

In terms of the business cycle, the retail sales series is best termed a "coincident indicator." However, its cyclical volatility is not great; consumer purchases, especially nominal purchases given their inclusion of inflation, can often continue to rise even after a recession has begun. On an annual basis, retail sales have never declined. The smallest annual rise (0.9 percent) came in 1991. Furthermore, monthly retail sales typically increase even during recessions. The best way to relate retail sales to the business cycle is in terms of the rate of growth in sales on a month-to-month basis. Most months will show increases, but during a recession they will become smaller and the declines, although still the exception and not the rule, become greater in frequency. (See Figures 22–2a, 22–2b, and 22–3.)

Weekly and Monthly Chain Store Sales

Since consumption accounts for two-thirds of real GDP, it is paramount to monitor the consumer closely. To this end, sales at the major retailers (such as Wal-Mart, Kmart, Sears, JC Penney, Dayton Hudson, Federated, etc.) provide a unique window on the consumer. Stock market participants have known this for years, and reports of stronger or weaker store sales have moved retail industry stock prices. However, the fixed-income markets now have become responsive to these data as well.

First, a little history is in order. Between the early 1960s and 1978, the Commerce Department compiled a weekly retail sales estimate for many of the sales categories currently available (e.g., food stores, furniture stores, etc.). Indeed, Federal Reserve Board Chairman Alan Greenspan was a big fan of that weekly series and once envisioned the day when a weekly GNP measure would be possible, with the centerpiece being weekly retail sales. But in that bygone age, these data commanded little market interest, and because of budget and statistical concerns the collection of weekly retail sales data ceased.

Sometime after the Commerce Department stopped the publication of their series, Edward Johnson, a retail equity analyst, began a weekly sales survey of the major retailers. His survey is part of an equity research product called the *Redbook Service*. As might be expected, Johnson's estimate of chain store sales is less comprehensive than the Commerce Department series. Moreover, the *Redbook* weekly sales estimate is based on year-over-year growth rate indications from the major chain stores instead of their sales revenues, which the Commerce Department was compiling. But to his credit, Ed Johnson fills a void for timely information on the consumer.

However, there are many pitfalls in compiling a weekly chain store sales growth-rate estimate. First, an assumption has to be made about market share. Second, the stores will not provide sales revenues on a weekly basis but only a growth rate indication. That indication, which might be a phrase similar to a "high single-digit gain," must be quantified. Third, some stores have unusual accounting periods though most of the major chains have daily internal reporting. Fourth, an implicit weight must be given to each week within the month. This can be a very tricky assumption around major holidays. After surmounting all of these problems, Johnson's estimate is grossed up by about 20 percent to represent total industry sales.

It is extremely important to recognize that these weekly *Redbook* data are subject to considerable volatility, which may be totally unimportant over the course of a given month due to special promotions, adverse or favorable weather, and other marketing events. Moreover, from Johnson's weekly sales estimate he also compiles a month-to-date average for the current four or five week sales accounting period, which is generally used throughout the industry. Additionally, that month-to-date estimate is seasonally adjusted and reported on a month-to-month basis. For the fixed-income markets, perceptions of consumer spending strength or weakness are formed on the basis of this month-to-month change.

Separately, the major retailers report sales revenue on a monthly basis. These company reports usually are available about a week before the Commerce Department releases data on retail sales for the comparable month. As a result, these store reports are also of interest to the markets. The monthly data can often successfully provide an indication of the change in Commerce Department's nonauto or general merchandise, apparel, and furniture store sales ("GAF" sales—which accounts for about 20 percent of total retail sales). But there are differences between the store sales data and the most comparable Commerce retail sales data. First, the chain store reports cover only publicly held companies that choose to report on a monthly basis, although by sales revenue this can account for 70–80 percent of GAF sales. Second, the accounting periods used by the retail industry (with some notable exceptions) often differ from a "true calendar month," on which the Commerce Department bases their measurement.

Statistically, between late 1989 and early 1992, the *Redbook* monthly retail sales estimate (which is an average of the weekly readings) explained 53 percent of the change in the Commerce Department's GAF sales, while a composite of monthly chain store sales revenue explained 68 percent of the change in the Commerce Department series. Consequently, if the goal is to forecast monthly retail sales, then the monthly chain store sales reports will prove a more accurate indication of the Commerce Department trends; but for timeliness, watch the weekly sales estimates.

Chapter 23

Unemployment Insurance Claims

General Description

The unemployment insurance (UI) program is a shared state and federal government-financed income-maintenance plan set up to help workers impacted by cyclical and temporary bouts of unemployment. The administration and eligibility requirements for collecting unemployment or jobless benefits are determined by each state. Consequently, coverage can vary by state. For example, some states, such as California, include agricultural workers, while most do not. Some states pay workers who are involved in a work stoppage, while most do not. Over time, the unemployment insurance program has included special longer term benefits, which have extended the duration of support for the unemployed up to twice the normal length of coverage. These programs have generally been legislated by Congress during or shortly after recessions. In 1991, Congress passed such a program, called the Emergency Unemployment Compensation Act of 1991 (Public Law 102-164). That act was amended late in that same year by Public Law 102-184, which established the Emergency Unemployment Compensation (EUC) Program, and these benefits were totally funded by the federal government. The EUC program was again amended in 1992 by Congress to increase the number of weeks of coverage. Much like the seven temporary and extended unemployment benefit programs that have preceded EUC over the last 30 years, this one served a timely need and will be eliminated when Congress believes that need has been met. (Currently the legislation allows the qualified unemployed to file under this program until October 1993).

Economic Indicator Information at a Glance

Market Significance	Moderate
Typical Release Time	8:30 AM Eastern Time Every Thursday
Released By	U.S. Department of Labor Employment and Training Administration
Period Covered	Prior Week Ending Saturday

Analyzing the Data

An initial claim for state unemployment insurance or jobless claim includes two types of claimants: (1) the first-time claimant during a benefit year, and (2) a repeat or "additional" claimant, who has filed previously and is again out of work. Some industries (such as the apparel industry) have an on/off work pattern, which might result in the same individual filing an initial claim every month for some "down time." Once an individual files for benefits, the individual's eligibility is checked. (During the year some states have noted that the percentage of individuals filing for benefits but who are ineligible has been as high as 40 percent.) An individual out of work for a strike may or may not qualify for jobless benefits, depending on the state and whether the work stoppage is a "lockout" or "walkout." But once an individual qualifies for benefits, the unemployed individual enters the ranks of the *continuing claimant* roll. Both series—the initial and continuing claims—provide an ongoing view of the labor markets. The jobless claim level and change provides the first indication of worsening or improving job markets. As such, it is the key focus of the financial markets. However, the continuing claims data provide a window on how quickly the labor markets can absorb the newly unemployed. For example, if the jobless claims pace accelerates but the continuing claims level holds steady, it suggests the duration of unemployment is rather short. However, the reverse is also true. If the pace of jobless

FIGURE 23–1a Initial Jobless Claims

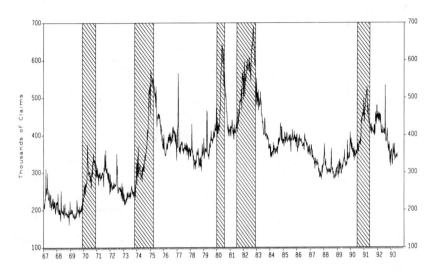

FIGURE 23–1b Initial Claims for State Unemployment Insurance
(January 1948–December 1992, Level)

Period	Historic Low	Normal Bounds			Historic High	Series Characteristics		
		Normal Low	Average	Normal High		Standard Deviation	Share of Total Observations	
Recession	229 K in Aug 1953	341 K	395 K	450 K	653 K in Sep 1992	109 K	96	18.1%
Recovery	222 K in May 1955	329 K	365 K	401 K	531 K in Dec 1982	72 K	123	23.3%
Expansion	166 K in Mar 1951	245 K	280 K	316 K	455 K in Sep 1992	71 K	310	58.6%

claims is relatively low but the continuing claims pace continues to rise, then the duration of unemployment is lengthening, which typically happens in the early stages of a business cycle expansion. (See Figures 23–1a, 23–1b, and 23–2.)

The interpretation of these data depends on several factors: (1) whether or not an emergency/extended benefit program is in effect, since those individuals filing under special programs are not counted in the *regular* program, which is the focus of the financial market's attention; (2) whether there was a holiday during the given filing period, which, despite the best efforts of the BLS to seasonally adjust these data, could still have a noticeable impact on the weekly change; and (3) whether the week is

FIGURE 23–2 Continuing Claims

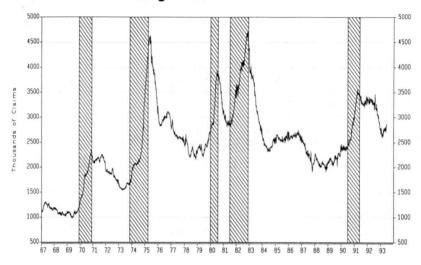

the first or second week of a new quarter, which can result in a "turn-of-the-quarter" upward blip in claims. In some cases, it benefits the individual who is unemployed late in a given quarter to wait until the beginning of the subsequent quarter to file for benefits in order to include the prior quarter wages in the calculation of the wage base for UI compensation. (4) Adverse weather can impact these data, as construction workers and agricultural workers could be temporarily laid off. (5) Legal changes to the state eligibility rules also could result in changes in the filing pace, which is a reason that is cited for the longer term downward trend of these data.

Because of the short-term "noise" in these data, a four-week moving average of the data is often more informative of the trends and should be looked at for conformation of any nascent trend. Additionally, the states often provide explanatory comments on why their state's claims rose or fell. Although this information is lagged one additional week from the current aggregate data, it still is useful for signs of sector and regional weakness.

Jobless Claims over the Business Cycle

Jobless claims are a timely and sensitive measure of labor market conditions, and they are classified as a leading economic indicator of general business conditions. During recessions, the average increase in the pace of filings is 15,000 per month, with an average level of about 400,000 claims. During recoveries the pace of filings tends to decline by about 10,000 per month and average about 365,000 claims. During expansions the improvement is slow—an average decline of about 500 claims per month, with the average filing rate during expansions dropping to 280,000 claims over the entire expansion.

Special Factors, Limitations, and Other Data Issues

Probably one of the key misunderstandings in using the initial claims data to project payroll employment changes is that in most states individuals must wait one week before filing. This "wait period" is often missed in relating the initial claim pace to monthly payroll employment changes.

Relationship with Other Series

Analysts often look to the weekly filings of unemployment claims and continuing jobless benefits as a guide to upcoming monthly employment and unemployment changes. But the statistical relationships are less reliable than might be desired. Indeed, between 1985–1992, the level or change in initial claims (new claimants) or state benefits (continuing beneficiaries), at best, explained only 20 percent of the monthly change in employment. So although it is a guide, it is by no means assured to improve one's employment forecast.

On a monthly basis, initial claims for unemployment insurance are included as a component of the composite index of leading indicators. This version of the data is not simply the monthly average of the weekly claims data, but it is used in the leading indicator as true month average with some conceptual adjustments.

References

Gary Burtless, "Unemployment Insurance and Labor Supply: A Survey," *Unemployment Insurance: The Second Half Century*, ed. W. Lee Hansen and James F. Byers, Madison, Wisc., University of Wisconsin Press, 1990, pp. 69–107.

Employment and Training Administration, U.S. Department of Labor, *An Examination of Declining UI Claims During the 1980s*, Occasional Paper 88-3, 1988.

Daniel N. Price, "Unemployment Insurance, Then and Now, 1935–85," *Social Security Bulletin*, October 1985 (Vol. 48, No. 10), pp. 22–32.

The Federal Reserve and the U.S. Treasury

Chapter 24

Overview

As important as it is to have a full understanding of business conditions indicators, the financial side of the equation plays just as crucial a role in the determination of financial market behavior, whether it's equities, foreign exchange, or the fixed income markets. For as much as one may completely understand how the economy is performing, it will serve little purpose if that knowledge is not properly utilized to project possible policy actions, particularly those of the Federal Reserve. It is all too often that financial markets accurately interpret data that show a change in the economic fundamentals but react little (if any) because it believes (properly or otherwise) that regardless of what the numbers say about the economy, they will not lead to a change in monetary policy.

The following sections deal with money supply, the Federal Reserve, and how the U.S. Treasury finances its debt. The discussion on money supply could just as easily come under the business conditions section. However, since it serves as the target variable for the Federal Reserve and can be considered the actual link between the Federal Reserve and the economy, it has been incorporated in this section. Needless to say, some market participants consider it *the* most important economic variable to watch. A view of the Federal Reserve is presented in two parts. The first provides an overview of the Federal Reserve decision-making process and the framework in which it conducts monetary policy. The second is a closer look at the mechanism often used to actually turn policy changes into interest rate changes. Finally, there is an overview of the U.S. Treasury's financing process. A steady supply of government issues is a given in the current environment of huge government deficits. To the extent that supply of a commodity can affect its price, familiarity with the government's pattern of bringing supply to the market is a necessary underpinning for understanding price changes of government securities.

Chapter 25

The Monetary Aggregates

General Description

Regardless of whether one is a monetarist or not, the fundamental premise that "money matters" is shared by all schools of economic thought. There are differences of opinion as to the magnitude of its impact, the channels through which it works, and its relative importance, but one really can't develop a macroeconomic model without money entering into the process.

Economic Indicator Information at a Glance

Market Significance	Varies Sharply
Typical Release Time	4:30 PM Eastern Time Thursday
Released By	Federal Reserve Board
Period Covered	Prior Week Ending Monday

Of course, that doesn't mean the issue is settled. One then has to define money. Thirty years ago, that was relatively simple; cash was cash, a check was drawn on a checking account, and in order to earn interest you put money in a local savings account. The lines were drawn distinctly. But through the 1970s, the 1980s, and now again in the 1990s, the lines became a blur and are now a burgeoning smudge. Legislative changes, financial innovation, and competition have spawned new deposit categories and an increasingly sophisticated investor base that is constantly learning of new products and willing to move its assets into investments that it had never heard of six months earlier. Adding to the problem is the fact that over the last 10 years interest rate levels have changed dramatically. In the early 1980s, the federal funds rate broke 19 percent, the 30-year bond yielded over 14.5 percent, and the spread between three-month bills and 30-year bonds reached -360 basis points. Through the ensuing decade, rates moved erratically to where at one point the federal funds rate was at 3.25 percent, 30-year bonds yielded about 7.50 percent, and the three-month bill to 30-year bond spread was +425 basis points. The drop in yields and the almost 800-basis-point swing in the yield spread created a plethora of changes in investment needs and options that had (and are still having) direct effects on money, however defined.

It is with consideration of this ever-changing environment that a rather straightforward presentation of the aggregates will be made. Fundamental points about the longer run viability of currently defined aggregates will highlight the problems created over the last 30 years. Although money may seem adequately defined at a given point in time, the existence of ongoing changes in the financial world make it likely that such a situation, at least for the foreseeable future, will wind up having been temporary.

The Monetary Aggregates

The Federal Reserve currently defines three monetary aggregates. Theoretically, they are ranked in terms of liquidity, or the degree to which they are transactions oriented. Practically speaking, the aggregates are also based on how well various combinations of deposit categories have tracked economic activity.

M1: The narrowest of aggregates is composed of actual hard currency held by the public (nondepository institutions), demand deposits, and traveler's checks. Demand deposits include normal checking accounts as well as interest-bearing checking accounts, collectively called other "checkable deposits." They are broken down into those held at commercial banks and at thrift institutions. As one can see, this is the most transactions-oriented monetary aggregate, and in theory it would look to be the aggregate most closely associated with economic activity. For this reason, when the Federal Reserve in 1970 moved from targeting bank credit to targeting money growth (as its intermediate target), it chose M1 as the policy focus. It held this preeminent position until 1983. Over the prior few years, financial deregulation and the high rate structure of the early 1980s caused the relationship between M1 and economic activity and inflation to deteriorate sharply.

FIGURE 25–1 M1–GDP Correlation Matrix

Nominal GDP Growth and M1 Growth 1960–1991			
1960–69	**1960–69**	**1970–79**	**1980–81**
GDP to M1	.795	.835	.011
GDP to M1 lag*	.603	.323	.319

*M1 growth lagged one year.

As a result, the Federal Reserve replaced M1 as the prime policy focus with the broader M2 aggregate. Since then M1 has continued to be a less than reliable monetary indicator of nominal economic activity. (See Figures 25–1 and 25–2.)

FIGURE 25–2 M1 Compositional Breakdown: End of 1992

Other Checkables	37.5%
Demand Deposits	33.2%
Currency	28.5%

M2: It is a large step from M1 to M2 in terms of size and of the disparity of the qualitative aspects of its components. Whether or not M1 adequately reflects economic activity at any given point in time, its role as a measure of transactions accounts is largely fulfilled. M2, however, enters that nebulous area of "near transactions accounts." Its current formulation reflects the idea that an aggregate's composition should not only be based on similar characteristics, but also on how well the combination of components shows a stable, long-term relationship with nominal economic activity.

All the aggregates build on each other, so in addition to M1, M2 includes general purpose and broker-dealer money market funds, overnight Eurodollar accounts, overnight repurchase agreements, small time deposits, and savings accounts.[1] It is more than triple the size of M1. The savings deposits and small time deposits are broken down further into those held at commercial banks and at thrift institutions. (See Figure 25–3.)

FIGURE 25–3 M2: Compositional Breakdown: End of 1992*
(Shares)

Savings Deposits	34%
M1	29
Small Time Deposits	25
Money Market Funds (General Purpose and Broker/Dealer)	10
Overnight Repurchase Agreements	1.5
Overnight Eurodollars	0.6

*Components and total are seasonally adjusted except for overnight eurodollars and repurchase agreements. This and rounding account for figures not adding to 100%.

M2 includes deposits that possess varying degrees of liquidity. Check writing privileges are granted for money market funds and the money market deposit accounts within savings deposits. They are very much akin to M1 deposits. From here, though, the degree of liquidity declines quickly. Overnight Eurodollars and repos are relatively liquid to the extent they represent one-day deposits. Even further removed from immediately spendable funds are savings accounts. They are readily accessible, but do not enjoy check writing privileges. Small time deposits really stretch the concept of an aggregate holding similarly liquid components. In fact, one has to consider them illiquid,

---

1   Savings accounts include money market deposit accounts, which essentially are bank money market funds.

given the penalties for early withdrawal. But the Fed had a different reason for including small time deposits; namely, their substitutability for savings accounts. Although not liquid, these deposits are a viable investment alternative for most of the other M2 components. It was thought best to include deposit categories that could readily capture deposits from the more liquid categories, so as not to have an aggregate whose volatility greatly exaggerated and potentially misrepresented the underlying monetary flows.[2]

As already mentioned, M2, until the mid-1980s, exhibited a fairly stable relationship with nominal GDP (see Figure 25–4). But its relationship also broke down and essentially crumbled in 1991–1992.

FIGURE 25–4 M2–GDP Correlation Matrix

Nominal GDP Growth and M2 Growth 1960–1991			
	1960–69	**1970–79**	**1980–91**
GDP/M2 lag*	.695	.691	.217

*M2 growth lagged one year.

Given the size and complexity of M2, it is important to stress the *long-term* nature of M2's statistical relationship to economic activity. Whereas one could make at least a theoretical case for M1 growth being closely related to nominal GDP growth over relatively short time periods (less than a year), such a case cannot be made for M2. M2 is more of a financial asset aggregate than it is a transactions aggregate. This very point was brought home to policy makers in 1991 and 1992. At that time, M2 growth was severely depressed by several factors. One was a significant shift out of lower yielding short-term deposits into bonds and mutual funds, neither of which is included in any

---

2   For a discussion of small time deposits role in M2, especially in light of the S&L crisis in the early 1990s, see John Wenninger and John Partlan, "Small Time Deposits and the Recent Weakness in M2," *Federal Reserve Bank of New York Quarterly Review*, Spring 1992, pp. 21–35. There is also a discussion of how the definitions of the aggregates evolved.

monetary aggregate. Another factor was the halt in bank lending, which made it unnecessary for financial institutions to attract funds into small time deposits in order to make loans.
Finally, the savings and loan debacle resulted in the closing of
thousands of thrifts. These institutions were the holders of significant amounts of small time deposits; and when they collapsed, a portion of those deposits were placed in non-M2 assets.

P*: M2 and INFLATION

In 1989, the Federal Reserve Board released a study[†] of the long-
term relationship between M2 and the price level in the United
States. It contended that the level of M2 was a reliable *long-term*
guideline for inflation if we were given M2's trend velocity and
the economy's potential trend GDP growth rate. The former was
considered stable over the long term (this century) and the latter
could be statistically formulated. With these two assumptions, a
given level of M2 could be used to project a given long-run equilibrium price level. This price level was designated P* (called
P star) and the study contended that when P* was running over
the current price level it portended accelerating inflation.

P* was a concept that greatly interested Federal Reserve Chairman Alan Greenspan (and consequently the financial markets) in
the early 1990s. But even the paper itself recognized that the P*
concept was not a reliable predictor of inflation over the short
run; in this instance, the short run could mean five years. Furthermore, the idea that M2's velocity was stable was severely
tested in 1992, when M2's growth rate and subsequent velocity
changed dramatically.

Its importance to the market and policy makers waned, as a
result.

[†]"M2 per Unit of Potential GNP as an Anchor for the Price Level." Hallman, Porter,
and Small. *Federal Reserve Bulletin*, April 1989.

M3: The broadest monetary aggregate includes M2, as well as
large time deposits (those for more than $100,000), term repurchase agreements, term Eurodollars, and institutional money
market funds. It is roughly 15 to 20 percent larger than M2.

FIGURE 25–5 M3: Compositional Breakdown: End of 1992*
(Shares)

M2	84%
Large Time Deposits	8.6
Institutional Money Market Funds	4.9
Term Repurchase Agreements	1.9
Term Eurodollars	1.1

*M3 total, large time deposits, and institutional money market funds are seasonally adjusted. Term repurchase agreements and eurodollars are not. This and rounding could cause figures to not add to 100 percent.

Since M2 comprises the bulk of M3 (See Figure 25–5), unlike the relationship of M1 and M2, the informational value of M3 is somewhat limited. The behavior of M2, for the most part, will dictate the behavior of M3. The value added is limited to information about large time deposits at commercial banks. These deposits have a stronger relationship with commercial and industrial loans made by banks than any other monetary aggregate component because they constitute a major source of funding for banks. In this sense, they can be an important variable to watch. During the period 1990 through 1992, while commercial and industrial loans at commercial banks were declining by about 14 percent, large time deposits dropped an even sharper 28 percent.

Beyond this, however, M3 adds little to the analysis of monetary growth and economic activity. For this reason, M3 has never been the focus of monetary policy. Even with volatile financial flows and the accompanying uncertainty about which aggregate is best as an indicator of monetary policy, it is unlikely it will ever be the preeminent aggregate.

Other Monetary Policy Indicators

The monetary aggregates are the most obvious focal point of monetary policy. But some prefer to use other means to gauge the stance of monetary policy. The two most commonly used alternative measures are the monetary base and Federal Reserve bank credit.

Monetary Base

The Federal Reserve's monetary base is defined as "total reserves plus the currency component of the money stock plus the portion of the cash held in banks' vaults that is not applied toward reserve requirements." At the end of 1992, the currency component accounted for about 83 percent of the monetary base, total reserves about 15 percent, and excess vault cash about 2 percent. As one can see, there should be a close relationship between M1 and the base, since most reserves are held against M1 deposits and currency is common to both M1 and the monetary base.

The rationale for focusing on the monetary base is that the components are considered the raw material from which money supply is created. The Fed, in theory, creates reserves and hard currency, so if one wants to ascertain what the Fed is up to, one should watch the monetary base, not the money supply.

Federal Reserve Bank Credit

A second alternative gauge of monetary policy is Federal Reserve bank credit, which is primarily the Federal Reserve's hold-

FIGURE 25–6 Federal Reserve Credit

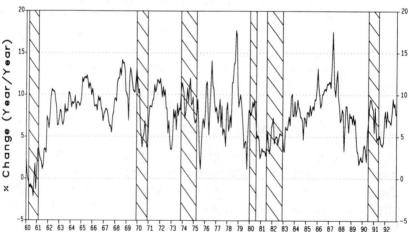

Note: Shaded areas represent business cycle recessions

FIGURE 25–7a Federal Reserve Bank's Monetary Base

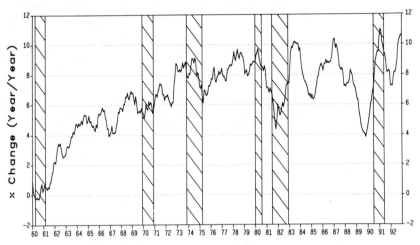

Note: Shaded areas represent business cycle recessions

FIGURE 25–7b Federal Reserve Bank's Monetary Base
(February 1959–December 1992, Simple annualized Month-to-Month Percentage)

Period	Historic Low	Normal Bounds			Historic High	Series Characteristics	
		Normal Low	Average	Normal High		Standard Deviation	Share of Total Observations
Recession	−4.5% in Dec 1960	+4.4 %	+6.3%	+8.2 %	+18.9% in Jan 1991	3.9 pp.	67	16.5%
Recovery	−4.6% in Jan 1981	+5.2 %	+7.0%	+8.8 %	+16.2% in Jun 1975	3.6 pp.	95	23.3%
Expansion	−3.8% in Oct 1959	+4.5 %	+6.2%	+7.9 %	+16.9% in Dec 1986	3.5 pp.	245	60.2%

ings of government securities. They account for about 90 percent of Federal Reserve bank credit, with close to 9 percent accounted for by other assets, such as foreign currencies. The data can be found in the Federal Reserve's H4.1 release, issued weekly at 4:30 p.m. on Thursdays.

For some observers, it is the first component that is critical, since Federal Reserve bank credit is considered the balance sheet manifestation of what is commonly called "monetizing the debt." Actually, it could be characterized as such although the phrase carries rather ominous, negative connotations of a proc-

FIGURE 25–8a Money Supply: M1

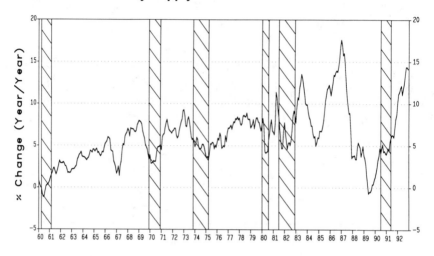

Note: Shaded areas represent business cycle recessions

FIGURE 25–8b Money Supply: M1
(February 1959–December 1992, Simple Annualized Month-to-Month Percentage)

Period	Historic Low	Normal Bounds			Historic High	Series Characteristics		
		Normal Low	Average	Normal High		Standard Deviation	Share of Total Observations	
Recession	−17.0% in Apr 1980	+1.7 %	+4.9%	+8.1%	+22.3% in Oct 1982	6.5 pp.	67	16.5%
Recovery	−12.5% in Dec 1980	+4.7 %	+7.4%	+10.1%	+21.7% in Aug 1982	5.3 pp.	95	23.3%
Expansion	−9.3% in May 1981	+2.7 %	+5.6%	+8.5%	+30.6% in Dec 1986	5.9 pp.	245	60.2%

ess that is strictly technical in nature. When the Fed needs to supply permanent reserves to the banking system, it does so by buying Treasury securities. But the timing and frequency of these purchases are determined by the banking system's demand for reserves. These purchases are not conducted arbitrarily and do not reflect changes in monetary policy. (A further discussion of these purchases is in Chapter 27.) Regardless, for some the purported monetization aspect of these purchases signifies underlying money creation, making Federal Reserve bank credit a monetary indicator worth watching. The fact that the Fed's purchases of Treasury securities is due to reserve demand

FIGURE 25–9a Money Supply: M2

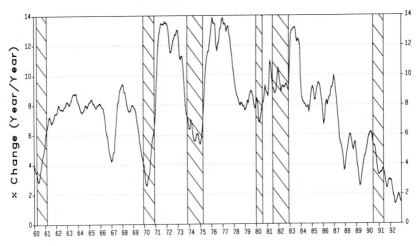

Note: Shaded areas represent business cycle recessions

FIGURE 25–9b Money Supply: M2
(February 1959–December 1992, Simple Annualized Month-to-Month Percentage)

Period	Historic Low	Normal Bounds			Historic High	Series Characteristics	
		Normal Low	Average	Normal High		Standard Deviation	Share of Total Observations
Recession	−6.1% in Feb 1970	+4.9 %	+6.9%	+8.9%	+16.1% in Jul 1980	4.0 pp.	67	16.5%
Recovery	−1.9% in Jun 1992	+6.4 %	+9.2%	+12.0%	+33.9% in Jan 1983	5.5 pp.	95	23.3%
Expansion	−0.4% in Feb 1989	+5.3 %	+6.9%	+8.5%	+15.5% in Jul 1972	3.3 pp.	245	60.2%

and therefore M1 growth, results in a relatively close set of relationships between Federal Reserve bank credit, reserves, and M1. (See Figures 25–6, 25–7a, and 25–7b.)

Money Supply over the Business Cycle

There are more similarities than differences between growth of the three monetary aggregates over the course of the business cycle. All show peak growth rates prior to the onset of a recession and growth low points before the end of the recession.

FIGURE 25–10a Money Supply: M3

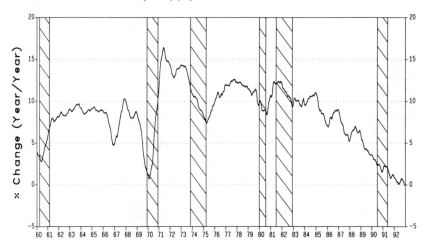

Note: Shaded areas represent business cycle recessions

FIGURE 25–10b Money Supply: M3
(February 1959–December 1992, Simple Annualized Month-to-Month Percentage)

| Period | Historic Low | Normal Bounds | | | Historic High | Series Characteristics | |
		Normal Low	Average	Normal High		Standard Deviation	Share of Total Observations
Recession	−4.5% in Feb 1970	+5.8 %	+8.0%	+10.2%	+17.7% in Sep 1970	4.4 pp.	67	16.5%
Recovery	−2.8% in Jun 1992	+6.3 %	+8.7%	+11.1%	+18.6% in Feb 1971	4.9 pp.	95	23.3%
Expansion	−3.7% in Aug 1969	+5.7 %	+7.6%	+9.5%	+16.1% in Aug 1972	3.9 pp.	245	60.2%

(This characteristic has led to the M2 aggregate being included in the composite index of leading indicators.) In terms of actual growth rates, all three aggregates experience their fastest growth during the recovery stage, with M2 actually averaging the same rate of growth during recessions as during expansions. (See Figures 25–8a, 25–8b, 25–9a, 25–9b, 25–10a, and 25–10b.)

Chapter 26

Monetary Policy: The Decision-Making Process

The Decision-Making Bodies

Monetary policy is determined by two operational bodies: the Federal Reserve Board (FRB) and the Federal Open Market Committee (FOMC). The Federal Reserve Board is *the* "monetary authority," although in practice the duties of each overlap when it comes to monetary policy—a point made apparent by the fact that the members of the FRB are automatically members of the FOMC. The FRB's decision-making scope goes beyond monetary policy into inter alia, banking regulation, while the FOMC's jurisdiction is solely in the monetary policy arena.

The Federal Reserve Board. The FRB is composed of seven members, appointed by the president. Terms run for 14 years, with the chairman and the vice chairman being appointed for four-year periods. If a member resigns, the replacement fulfills the remainder of the term rather than starting a new one. In making the appointments, the president is supposed to take into consideration the Federal Reserve districts in which existing members preside or were "elected from." The idea is to have diverse geographical representation on the board. The Senate must approve all FRB appointments.

Federal Open Market Committee. Commonly referred to as the FOMC, the committee is composed of 12 members, the seven members of the FRB and five presidents chosen from the 12 Federal Reserve districts. The president of the New York Federal Reserve Bank is always a sitting member. The remaining four seats rotate on an annual basis from among the remaining 11 districts.

How Policy Is Made

Although there is no real "starting point" for monetary policy, one convenient place to begin for our purposes is with the first installment of the chairman of the Federal Reserve's semi-annual Humphrey-Hawkins testimony. It is then—the testimony is presented to the House and Senate Banking Committees typically in February—that the FRB and the district Federal Reserve presidents set forth their goals for growth in the money supply, their projections for economic activity and for inflation, their overall sense of how the economy will fare, and what problems the economy may face in the coming year.

It is a broad agenda, with the only policy specifics being monetary targets. The year's goals for money supply are set in accordance with the Full Employment and Balanced Budget Act of 1978, the legislation that mandated that the Federal Reserve chairman testify before Congress twice a year. The second time is the mid-year review in July, at which time the targets are reevaluated and altered if deemed prudent, and preliminary money targets are set for the following year. All growth and inflation forecasts are just that, forecasts, and should not be considered policy targets.

Macroeconomic Policy

For our purposes, macromonetary policy will be defined as "the setting of targets for the nation's money supply." Actually, it begins with the determination of which money supply to target, M1 or M2 or M3, or possibly even a broad credit aggregate. The parameters for choosing a particular aggregate or group of aggregates are various, but they certainly include how the aggregate has behaved in previous years and what has been the relationship between a particular aggregate and economic activity and inflation. These factors will be explored fully in the upcoming discussion of the aggregates; for now, though, we will assume the Fed has chosen which aggregate(s) it is targeting for the year.

In setting its monetary targets, the Fed has two goals in mind. One is to allow for the economy to grow at an acceptable rate, and the other is to ensure this growth is accompanied by an acceptable inflation rate. Current Fed policy, and one that has not necessarily been followed in the past or will be followed in the future, is geared towards setting monetary targets that will result over time in a slow downward move in the inflation rate. This desire is signaled by lowering the monetary growth targets over a number of years. For example, the stated growth target for M2 for 1993 is a range of +2 percent to +6 percent. In 1985 the target range was +6 percent to +9 percent. Without exploring fully the theoretical underpinnings, it is sufficient to say that the generally held belief "that inflation essentially is a monetary phenomenon" is the driving force behind this long-term policy position. In fact, it is this belief that guides many Federal Reserve policy makers to deem that fighting inflation is the Federal Reserve's primary, if not sole, function.

Once these targets have been set, the Federal Reserve gets down to the day-to-day business of trying to meet its goals. It is then that the interplay between the Federal Reserve Board and the Federal Open Market Committee attempts to resolve the economic issues that affect monetary growth.

Day-to-Day Operations—The FOMC

Most of the operational details of monetary policy are conducted under the auspices of the Federal Open Market Committee. Formal meetings take place about every five to eight weeks and typically occur for one day. Two-day meetings were relatively common in the early to mid-1980s but now seemingly are confined to meetings immediately preceding the two Humphrey-Hawkins testimonies. The discussions are very wide ranging, covering all aspects of economic activity. Fed staffers present forecasts for economic growth, inflation, and money supply growth. The committee members and the other Federal Reserve presidents discuss the current economic situation in detail, evaluating statistical and anecdotal evidence. Various specific issues can be brought to the fore (e.g., the U.S. dollar, if it is appreciating or depreciating quickly). Given the size of the committee, disagreement is only natural; diverse opinions are held on most subjects. After the committee has discussed all issues it considers pertinent to monetary policy for the upcoming inter-meeting period, a consensus is reached as to how monetary policy is to be conducted in the upcoming intermeeting period. A vote is then taken in support of the directive that outlines the consensus view. Votes against the directive are not uncommon, but are usually offered by only by a few FOMC members. The most common reasons for votes against the directive are the action or bias prescribed by the directive, although differences of opinion as to what variables to focus on can be a source of contention as well. This directive, which is issued to the Federal Reserve Bank of New York, the district bank responsible for the day-to-day implementation of monetary policy, sets forth the committee's expectations for money growth over the next quarter, typically reaffirms the Fed's longer term monetary goals, and sets a strategy for policy until the next meeting.

What Is the Fed Up To?
The FOMC Minutes, Beige Book, and
Bank Lending Survey

Changes in Federal Reserve policy can be gleaned from its open market operations. But information as to how the FOMC's collective thought process is evolving and what information the FOMC is receiving is crucial also.

The first place to start is with the FOMC minutes. They are released at 4:30 p.m. on the Friday after an FOMC meeting, and they cover the meeting prior to the one just conducted. Thus, there is an information lag in their publication, since approximately six weeks will have lapsed since the meeting. A lot can happen in that period of time. Be that as it may, one can still catch the flavor of the committee's thought process by reading the minutes. One can ascertain how much agreement there was regarding policy at the time of the prior meeting, what economic variables the committee was stressing, and whether or not policy changes were in the air then and how that would extrapolate to the present.

One additional nuance one can see is the committee's bias for policy actions until the next meeting. It is not unusual for the FOMC to be inclined to move policy in one direction or the other. This is called adopting an "asymmetric" policy directive. In the case of a bias towards tightening, it would be worded as follows "... slightly greater reserve restraint would be acceptable while slightly lesser reserve restraint might be acceptable...." The key is the choice of *would* versus *might*; *would* is considered a stronger policy usage than *might*. If the Fed were neutral in terms of potential policy changes it would adopt a so-called *symmetric* directive and say that greater or lesser restraint *would* [both] be acceptable.

The beige book, or tan book, is a summary provided for the FOMC meeting by each of the 12 Federal Reserve districts that conveys the state of the economy, growth and inflation, in each district. It is released at noon on Wednesday, two weeks prior to the FOMC meeting. Usually, the beige book carries few surprises. Its information typically mirrors what actual economic statistics have already revealed.

Another piece of information made available is the Federal Reserve's quarterly survey of bank lending practices or the Senior Bank Lending Officer's Survey. Started in 1990, when commercial banks were under increasing financial strain and bank loans were on the decline, it reflects information from approximately 58 banks about, inter alia, their standards for approving credit and whether or not loan growth is increasing or decreasing and in what sector or type of loan.

The strategy is set forth in the context of the current state of policy. That is, the directive instructs the New York Fed, via the open market desk, to maintain the existing policy stance, to move in a particular direction, or even more common, to bias potential policy changes during the intermeeting period in a particular direction.

Policy Changes

Whereas monetary policy is set in terms of broad inflation and growth goals and specific monetary targets, an actual policy shift does not deal directly with these areas. Particularly, the Fed currently does not change its monetary targets as a primary means of altering policy. The main mechanism is a change in short-term interest rates.[1] Federal Reserve monetary policy, via FRB or FOMC decisions, can directly affect two interest rates: the discount rate and the federal funds rate. It is responsible for setting the discount rate, the overnight rate at which the Fed lends to member banks, while the FOMC exerts a very strong influence over the federal funds rate, the overnight rate at which banks lend to each other.

The decision to change the discount rate or change reserve requirements is made by the Federal Reserve Board. A change in the federal funds rate, the most often used policy mechanism, is decided upon by the FOMC. The first policy mechanism is considered a bolder, more overt move, signaling an aggressive policy change. For monetary policy makers, it is a "sit up and take notice" change given to the public at large and the financial markets. A change in the federal funds rate is the more commonly employed policy tool and can, if desired, affect interest rates by the same amount as a change in the discount rate. Even so, a change in the federal funds rate is considered a quieter, more subtle way to affect interest rates. One only has to note that a change in the discount rate usually makes the front page of newspapers, while a change in the federal funds rate typically is consigned to the business section and usually the credit market section to get a sense of the difference.

Once a policy change is effected, it is up to the financial markets to carry out the Fed's game plan. Though general market rates, Treasury bill and note and bond rates, and all other short- and long-term interest rates are not tied directly to the federal funds rate, they are loosely linked via the term structure effect—

---

1   A second tool, but historically one that has been used infrequently, is a change in reserve requirements. During the banking sector difficulties in the 1990–1992 period, this mechanism was employed twice. In December 1990, the FRB cut the reserve requirements on net eurodollar liabilities and nonpersonal time deposits with maturity of less than one and one-half years from 3 percent to zero. In February 1992, the FRB cut the reserve requirement on transaction deposits from 12 percent to 10 percent. Ostensibly, both cuts were undertaken to increase bank lending and shore up bank profitability. Since this policy lever is not commonly employed, all future references to policy shifts will pertain strictly to interest rate changes.

overnight rates are implicitly built into one-month rates, which are built into three-month rates, and on and up the interest rate maturity chain (See Figure 26–1).[2] As Figure 26-2 indicates, the effect on market interest rates of a change in the federal funds rate is less and less the further one goes out the yield curve.

FIGURE 26–1 The Interest Rate Chain

Discount →	Federal →	Treasury Bill →	Treasury →	Treasury
Rate	Funds Rate	Rates	Note Rates	Bond Rates

Be that as it may, the guiding principle of monetary policy as conducted by the Federal Reserve is to rely on interest rate changes to affect economic growth, inflation, and the money supply. And that effect can be quite strong. But again, the Fed has no control over the extent to which, or the time frame in which, changes in the discount rate or federal funds rate are transferred to market interest rates, especially long-term interest rates. Another look at Figure 26–2 also shows that the correlation between the federal funds rate and Treasury rates falls with shorter periodicities (i.e., months versus quarters), especially as one moves further out the yield curve. Still, the rather high degree of correlation shows that the Fed's policy mechanism is by no means a hit or miss prospect. But a host of other factors (supply and demand conditions and even financial market psychology) have important effects also.

As imperfect as this mechanism is, though, it has worked time and time again. With that in mind, it is worth exploring the exact manner in which the Federal Reserve goes about altering the discount rate and the federal funds rate. The former is relatively easy. The Fed just announces a change in the discount

---

2   For a discussion of the term structure of interst rates, refer to any standard monetary policy or financial market textbook, such as Frederic S. Mishkin *Economics of Money, Banking and Financial Markets*, Second Edition, Glenview, IL, Scott Foresman Inc.,1989.

Chapter 26

FIGURE 26–2 Yield Curve Correlation: The Federal Funds Rate and Treasury Rates: 1980 to 1990, Quarterly

	3-Month Treasury Bill	One-Year Treasury Bill	Five-Year Treasury Note	Ten-Year Treasury Note	Thirty-Year Treasury Bond
Federal Funds Rate	.990	.971	.883	.849	.815

Yield Curve Correlation: The Federal Funds Rate and Treasury Rates: 1980 to 1990, Monthly

	3-Month Treasury Bill	One-Year Treasury Bill	Five-Year Treasury Note	Ten-Year Treasury Note	Thirty-Year Treasury Bond
Federal Funds Rate	.981	.953	.848	.805	.771

rate, since it sets the rate. However, when a change in the federal funds rate is deemed to be the proper policy response, the mechanism is much more complicated. Since the federal funds rate is a market interbank rate, the Fed cannot ordain its level. But the federal funds market is a market for bank reserves. And since the Federal Reserve ultimately determines the supply of reserves within the banking system, it has a powerful tool for affecting the rate charged for federal funds. And how the Fed affects policy changes via its manipulation of the supply of reserves is the subject of our next chapter.

Chapter 27

Implementing Monetary Policy Directives: Open Market Operations

General Description

In a trader's perfect world, it would be best to know instantaneously of all decisions to alter monetary policy. In a sense, this does happen when there is a change in the discount rate. For all intents and purposes, the Federal Reserve Board decides upon and then quickly implements the change. And that change is overt—an announced reduction or increase in the discount rate. Unfortunately, one does not have an immediate view of the decision-making process for the vast majority of changes in monetary policy that are executed by the Federal Open Market Committee. Furthermore, the implementation of a policy change directive is not as clear-cut as a discount rate change, which is publicly announced. Instead, the new directive is put into place via open market operations. Technically, these are the day-to-day actions by which the Fed manages the supply of bank reserves. But also they are the way that the Federal Reserve translates a new directive into concrete action. An understanding of open market operations is critical to understanding fully how monetary policy works. It is the means for deciphering and determining most of the changes in monetary policy. In this context, it is important to be able to discern the difference between a technical open market operation and one that is signaling a policy change.

There are numerous ways in which the Federal Reserve can utilize open market operations to communicate its policy position. These methods have changed through the years and are more than likely going to change in the years to come. They have been altered during the regimes of particular Fed chairmen and are subject to change under a new chairman, when the composition of the board changes, or when economic conditions warrant a different approach to monetary policy.

A key point is that different approaches offer varying degrees of openness; that is, how well each method communicates the change in policy. Ultimately, we will provide two examples: current operating procedures and the procedure used immediately prior to current practice. This will provide a better flavor of monetary policy techniques and also offer better preparation for the next time the dictates of the Fed change, as they inevitably will. First though, there is the technical aspect of open market operations that must be addressed, for no matter what policy changes take place, they must be administered within the basic framework of the banking system's ongoing need for reserves. It is always within the context of this need that one has to determine whether or not monetary policy has been altered by the FOMC.

Open Market Operations: The Technicals

The most basic tenet of economics, demand and supply, is the cornerstone of the Federal Reserve's open market operations. These operations are defined here as the Fed's day-to-day management of bank reserves. As we shall see, this management effectively means trying to keep the supply of reserves in balance with demand at the desired federal funds rate. In some quarters, these operations are often considered to be the Fed's way of adding or draining liquidity from the system, and technically, that is the case. But as we shall see, the Fed could be trying to push interest rates higher when it "adds liquidity" or moving towards lower rates when it "drains liquidity." One should not confuse the technical aspects of open market operations with broader macroeconomic policy.

The Demand for Reserves

Recalling Economics 101 or your first course in monetary theory, the U.S. banking system is subject to a fractional reserve

system. That is, for every dollar a bank customer holds in transaction accounts, the bank must hold a fraction of that dollar "in
reserve." For the most part, that fraction is 3 percent.[1] So for
every dollar on deposit, a bank must hold 3 cents in reserve. In
reserve means either keeping 3 cents in its vaults, in cash, or
keeping it on deposit at its district Federal Reserve bank. These
reserves, for obvious reasons, are called "required reserves,"
and constitute the largest "demand" for reserves.

Required reserves are based on the average amount of deposits in a two-week period ending on a Monday and are held
during the two-week period ending on the following Wednesday. This 14 day Thursday-to-Wednesday period is called a "reserve," or "statement," or "maintenance" period. Thus, if a bank
had average deposits of $20 bn. in a particular statement period,
the bank would have to hold $600 mn., on average, over the
course of the two-week period. The bank does not have to hold
3 percent of each day's deposits, which can fluctuate wildly, on
that day or hold $600 mn. on each day. All it has to do is make
sure that its holdings of required reserves, average $600 mn. for
the two-week period. Thus, a bank could hold $600 mn. each
day or $8.4 bn. for one day and no reserves the remaining 13
days, and in each case would meet its legal requirement.

The other source of demand for reserves is called "excess
reserves." Deposit flows (by their nature) are volatile and unpre-
dictable. Furthermore, many smaller banks do not have the sophisticated systems necessary to monitor deposit flows closely.
As a result, banks, in the aggregate, will hold more reserves than
are necessary as a precaution against uncertain deposit changes.
On an absolute scale, these reserves are a very small portion of
the total demand for reserves, amounting to only about 2 percent. But at any given point in time, changes in the demand for
excess reserves can be as problematic for the Fed in determining
its open market operations as can be a change in any of the
other demand and supply factors.

---

1   Net transaction accounts of zero to $46.8 million have a reserve requirement of 3
    percent. Accounts of more than $46.8 mn. have a reserve requirement of 10
    percent.

These are the two sources of demand for reserves in the banking system and are so designated in the balance sheet below.

Reserves

Demand	Supply
Required Reserves	
Excess Reserves	

The Supply of Reserves

Similar to the demand side of the ledger, or of the balance sheet, there are two main sources of the "supply" of reserves. They are "borrowed reserves" and "nonborrowed" reserves. Banks can get reserves credited to their account at their district Fed by borrowing directly from the district Fed. This is borrowing at the discount window, and the discount rate is the rate charged for this privilege. All other sources of supply are called nonborrowed reserves, a catchall phrase for total reserves minus borrowed reserves. This source of funds constitutes about 98 percent of the reserves in the system, and the federal funds market is where these reserves are traded. The balance sheet is essentially complete:

Reserves

Demand	Supply
Required Reserves	Borrowed Reserves
Excess Reserves	Nonborrowed Reserves

Or in equation form:

Required Reserves + Excess Reserves = TOTAL RESERVES =

Borrowed Reserves + Nonborrowed Reserves

For now, the focus will turn to the nonborrowed reserve component. It is here that we find most of the factors that unpredictably affect the supply of reserves, create the greatest imbalances in the equilibrium of reserves, and induce the Federal Reserve to conduct its open market operations. The nonborrowed reserve factors are listed in the Federal Reserve's H4.1 release. Many of these factors do not show significant movement from week to week or statement period to statement period, but there are a few that account for the greatest volatility in reserve flows. Chief among these more volatile factors are float, Treasury balances at the Federal Reserve, currency in circulation, and other assets.

Float

"Float" is the timing gap between when a check is credited at the receiving bank and when it is finally debited at the paying bank. Essentially, two banks are using the same dollar. A bank to which a check is presented for payment receives credit for the amount of the check from the Federal Reserve, within two days of its being presented. However, it can take more than two days for that check to be debited against the bank on which it is drawn. Usually, inclement weather or a holiday delays the processing of the check and creates "transportation float." Thus, when processing is delayed, the paying bank still has the funds while the receiving bank is credited with the funds and can also use them to meet its required reserve need.

The important point is that an increase (decrease) in float temporarily increases (decreases) the supply of reserves within the banking system.

Treasury Balances at the Fed

The U.S. Treasury keeps its cash in two places—in tax and loan accounts (T&L) at depository institutions and in its account at the Federal Reserve. The former accounts must be collateralized; therefore, there is a limit to how much banks can or choose to accept. Lately the system-wide "limit" for T&L accounts has been around $35 bn. Overall, Treasury balances can vary widely, though, and in 1992 they ranged from $5.3 bn. to $58.8 bn.

The second depository for the government's funds is the Federal Reserve, the account from which the U.S. government pays its bills. The Treasury now attempts to keep its deposits at the Federal Reserve in the $5 bn. range, with the $7 bn. range the target after significant tax dates. But the actual amount is subject to great volatility due to the variability of tax receipts and government outlays. The fact that there is a limit to the amount that can be held in T&L accounts also is critical. At tax times (January, April, June, September and December), receipts can be so great that T&L limits are reached and all additional funds have to be deposited at Federal Reserve banks. At these times Treasury deposits at the Fed can soar to over $25 bn.

How does all of this affect the supply of reserves? When the Treasury processes a receipt and deposits it in a T&L account, all that happens is the funds are transferred from private sector accounts to a public account. Importantly, though, the funds still are in the private banking system. However, when the Treasury transfers funds to its Federal Reserve account, private banks no longer have access to the funds and cannot use them to meet reserve requirements. So when the Treasury deposits a receipt into its account at the Fed, the money is leaving the private banking system, and banks cannot utilize the money to meet reserve requirements. As can be seen, then, an increase (decrease) in Treasury balances at the Fed decreases (increases) the supply of reserves in the system.

Currency in Circulation

"Currency in circulation" is the amount of money held by the public in coin and paper. When cash and coin are held by a bank it is called "vault cash." As stated before, vault cash can be used to meet a bank's reserve requirements. When the public increases its demand for physical money (holiday periods typically show an increase in currency in circulation), it reduces the amount of reserves in the banking system either by reducing vault cash in the banking system or reducing banks, reserve accounts at the Fed when the banks go to the district Federal Reserve Bank to replenish their vault cash. Thus, the reserve impact is such that an increase (decrease) in currency in circulation decreases (increases) the supply of reserves.

Other Assets

Although it is not utilized in the example, there is another important reserve category worth mentioning; it's called "other assets." This component includes, among other things, the Federal Reserve's foreign currency holdings. It is through this category that foreign exchange intervention has an effect on open market operations. If the Fed is defending the dollar, it will buy dollars and sell foreign currencies. The dollars will flow into the Fed and out of the system, while the foreign currencies will enter the world's financial system. As one can see, the action of helping the U.S. dollar drains reserves from the system. In the opposite situation, in which the Fed is helping to prop up a foreign currency, the Fed would buy that currency, sell dollars, and thereby add reserves to the system.

Balancing the Supply and Demand for Reserves

With an understanding of the main components of the reserve equation, the next step is to look at the connection between the balance sheet and open market operations. To do so, a more detailed balance sheet is constructed with Treasury balances at the Fed, float and currency in circulation representing the supply of nonborrowed reserves.

One way to look at each demand and supply component is to determine the amount each factor changes from maintenance period to maintenance period. Thus, if float were $500 mn. in Period One and rose to $1.5 bn. in the subsequent period, $1 bn. more reserves are in the system in Period Two. This approach can be applied to each of the reserve factors. Similarly, if transactions deposits in the banking system rise from Period One to Period Two, so will required reserves. For now, we will assume that there is no change in the amount of reserves borrowed from the discount window and arbitrarily assign changes to each of the other balance sheet components.

Reserves

Demand		Supply	
Required Reserves	+2000	Borrowed Reserves	
Excess Reserves	+500	Nonborrowed Reserves	
		Float	+1000
		Treasury Balance @ Fed	+1000
		Currency in Circulation	+500

To make the analysis even easier, the balance sheet will be restructured so that one side will hold the factors that increase the supply of reserves (decreasing the demand for reserves would have the same effect) and the other side will hold the factors that reduce the supply of reserves (or increase the demand). As the factors are rearranged, remember that an increase in one factor, such as float, increases reserves in the system, while an increase in Treasury balances at the Fed decreases the amount of reserves in the system.

Reserves

Increase Supply		Decrease Supply	
Decrease Demand		Increase Demand	
Float	1000	Required Reserves	2000
Excess Reserves	500	Excess Reserves	500
		Treasury Balance at Fed	1000
		Currency in Circulation	500
Sum:	1000		4000

The assumption is that reserves were in balance in the previous period. The Fed then looks at the latest data and uses its internal forecasts to generate numbers like those above.[2] It shows that although float will rise and generate a surplus of reserves in the system, other factors will "take reserves out of the system." Banks are expected to be holding more deposits and thus will need to hold more required reserves. There also is forecasted a rise in banks' demand for excess reserves during the period. Furthermore, individuals are projected to desire more cash in hand and therefore reduce the supply of reserves in the banking system. As one can see, whether demand increases or supply falls, the effect is the same: there is a shortage of reserves in the banking system.

---

2   Technically, the Federal Reserve uses levels of reserves instead of changes, but the end result is the same.

Summing up each side, the net effect is that there is projected to be \$3 bn. too few reserves in the system in the upcoming statement period, either due to a reduction in supply or greater demand. If the situation were left unattended, demand would far exceed supply. As we learned in Micro 101, the "price" of those reserves would have to rise. In this case, that means the federal funds rate would increase—if the situation were left unattended.

The anticipation of a reserve imbalance, something that occurs in just about every maintenance period, creates the need for open market operations. As stated before, these operations are the Federal Reserve's tools for keeping the supply of and demand for reserves in balance. In this instance, the Fed would need to supply \$3 bn. of reserves to the banking system to insure a smoothly functioning market for bank reserves.

The Need to Add Reserves

The Federal Reserve has numerous ways to add reserves to the system. One is called a *customer repurchase agreement*, or customer repo. Foreign monetary and international authorities have a pool of dollars on deposit at the Federal Reserve. In order to earn interest on these dollar holdings, the authorities engage in repurchase agreements with the Fed. The importance of this pool is that these authorities are giving money to the Fed in exchange for securities (repurchase agreements). Similar to Treasury balances, if cash is in an account at the Fed, it is no longer in the banking system and cannot be used to meet reserve requirements. Thus, if this pool were to increase, money would be leaving the banking system and reserves would be drained from the system. A customer repo is when the Federal Reserve passes existing repos through to the primary dealer community. The key is *existing* repos. Thus, instead of the Fed doing the repo with the account of a foreign central bank or international authority, it is done with a primary dealer. And when it is done with a primary dealer the cash, instead of being on deposit at the Fed, goes back into the banking system via a primary dealer's account, adding reserves to the banking system.

A customer repo typically ranges in size from $700 mn. to $3 bn. There are no restrictions, per se, as to the size of a customer repo, except that it is limited by the size of the internal reverse pool (of which the Fed would not employ the total amount). There is no technical limit to the term of a customer repo, either, although 99.9 percent of the time a customer repo is conducted for one business day (including weekends). Once, in 1986, the Fed conducted a 15-day customer repo.

Another means by which the Federal Reserve can supply reserves is with a *system repo*. System repos are transactions directly between the Federal Reserve and primary dealers. The Fed gets the securities and the banking system gets the cash (reserves). What is the difference between a customer and system repo, besides the parties involved? The primary one is the size. System repos can almost always be assumed to be for a greater amount than customer repos. In a recent two-month period, the average customer repo conducted was for $1.6 bn., while the average size of an overnight system was $4.4 bn. An overnight repo can reach $10 bn. or more if necessary, and there is no limit to how large it can be. A second important difference is that system repos are often done for longer than one business day (or overnight). These are called *term repos*. Two-, three-, and four-day system repos are fairly common, with five- and seven-day repos also in the Fed's arsenal. Term repos are usually smaller than overnight repos. But at a recent average of $2.5 bn., they still are typically larger, and therefore add more reserves per day than a customer repo. One final difference is that the size of a customer repo is announced at the time it is conducted. The size of a system repo, however, is not known at the time it is conducted. Its size, or a close estimate of its size, has to be extracted from the subsequent H4.1 Federal Reserve statistical release.

The previous open market operations (customer and system repos) are both temporary means of adding reserves. In each case, the cash goes back into the Fed's coffers after the specified period of the repurchase agreement. However, the Fed can add reserves to the system permanently by buying securities, either Treasury bills or coupons. These outright purchases are called *bill or coupon passes*.

Passes are conducted when the add need is fairly large, approximately $4 bn. or greater, and when large add needs are projected for at least a couple of maintenance periods. The need for passes is very seasonal and usually can occur in April or June, or the August/September and November/December periods. During these times certain reserve factors combine to drain a large amount of reserves for an extended period of time.

Historically, the difference between a bill and a coupon pass was one of size. Bill passes typically were about $1 bn. to $2 bn. larger than coupon passes. But this is no longer the case. In 1992 three bill passes and three coupon passes were conducted, with the bill passes averaging $4.9 bn. and the coupon passes averaging $4.4 bn. In fact, one of the coupon passes was for more than $5 bn. What also has changed is the frequency of bill-versus-coupon passes. Whereas bill passes clearly had been the preferred instrument for adding permanent reserves in the 1980s (seven in a row between November 1989 and May 1991), most recent Fed behavior shows a distinct preference for coupon purchases over bill purchases. Part of this change is the Fed's stated effort to help lower long-term interest rates by increasing its purchases of longer dated Treasury securities.

Another means of adding reserves permanently is to purchase Treasury securities from the foreign accounts that hold a large pool of government securities and keep them at the Fed. These are referred to as "internal purchases." This can be considered an under-the-table operation. These purchases are typically modest relative to bill or coupon passes, amounting to several hundred million dollars instead of billions. They also typically are employed during periods of extended large needs and the Fed will often use them for a number of weeks in a row in lieu of, or in addition to, outright purchases.

For customer and system repos, the Federal Reserve announces the operation, currently between 11:30 a.m. to 11:35 a.m. Outright purchases also are publicly announced, but the announcement times vary. In 1992, 12:30 p.m. was a general center of gravity, but a bill pass was announced minutes before noon on one occasion. Internal purchases are not announced. Their presence can be gleaned only by calculations derived from the Fed's H4.1 statistical release.

Which Method to Use—Systems or Customers or Outright Purchases?

As can be inferred from the previous discussion, the choice of adding operations depends primarily on the size and duration of the add need. A rough rule of thumb is that customers are used for add needs of about $2.5 bn. or less. Add needs larger than that will be addressed with system repos or a mix of customers and systems, either overnight or term operations. But this refers to average add needs over the course of the two-week maintenance period. Also important is the size of the add need within the period. For instance, a given maintenance period may present an add need of only $1.5 bn. But it is important to know if that add need is spread evenly throughout the period, at $1.5 bn. per day, or concentrated over a shorter time period, say three days. In the former instance, a daily diet of $1.5 bn. customers would be appropriate. But under the latter circumstances, the add need becomes $7 bn. for those three days, and the choice of methods would be quite different. This is because the Fed tries to time its open market operations to coincide with the reserve flows. Thus, it typically would choose to conduct system repos worth $7 bn. for those three days, providing the liquidity when it was most needed. However, in each case, the amount added would be the same on a period average basis.

The Need to Drain Reserves

So far the only position studied was one in which there was a dearth of reserves. This is the situation in which the Fed finds itself most weeks of the year. But there are also times when there are too many reserves in the system. Remember that open market operations are geared towards maintaining an equilibrium in the reserve market. So when the reserve factors move to produce an overabundance of reserves, the Fed is forced to enter the market and conduct operations that drain reserves from the system. In terms of the previous example, all one would have to do is flip the sign on each of the factors. They would move to opposite sides of the balance sheet and create a situation in which there were $3 bn. too many reserves in the system.

The Fed reduces the supply of reserves in the banking system via operations that are the opposite of some of the operations it uses to add reserves, and one other that cannot be done to add reserves.

For all practical purposes, matched sale-repurchase agreements are the opposite of system repurchase agreements. The Fed receives cash from the banking system in exchange for securities. Technically, the transaction is not a reverse repo, but an agreement by the Fed to literally sell the securities outright and then buy them back on a specified date. The characteristics of matched sales are the same as a system repo in terms of length—overnights to extended terms—and size—anywhere from a few hundred million to over $10 bn. When a match sale operation is conducted, the Fed receives cash for the securities; thus, the money, or reserves, leave the banking system. The supply of reserves is thereby temporarily reduced.

Similar to a bill or coupon pass, the Fed can also drain reserves permanently via a bill sale. Coupon sales are not utilized by the Fed. Again the motivation is the same, a large extended need but one in which reserves in the system are in surplus. Such situations are very infrequent, with there being only one seasonal time, January/February, in which bill sales typically occur.

There are two "internal means" of draining reserves from the system as well. The counterpart to buying securities from the pool held by foreign accounts, and kept at the Fed, is to sell securities to these accounts. The Fed receives cash (reserves) which reduces the supply of reserves. The second way is for the Federal Reserve to roll off a portion of its own holdings of Treasury securities at the Treasury's bill auctions. The Fed has a large holding of Treasury securities, some of which mature at every auction. Normally, the Fed will replace its entire holdings of each maturing bill with the bill being auctioned. But if it chooses, the Fed can redeem a portion of those holdings for cash. In so doing, the Treasury pays the Federal Reserve cash and reserves move from the banking system to the Fed. This process has the same reserve effect as Treasury deposits at the Fed rising, although here the drain is permanent. There is nothing analogous to this on the add side because the Federal Reserve is not allowed legally to increase the size of its Treasury security holdings via the auction process.

Open Market Operations: Policy Implications

The previous discussion makes open market operations look very mechanical. And most times, they are. If policy is being held steady, there is little in the day-to-day machinations of customer repos, system repos, or matched sales that (in a broad market context) are particularly important. But when the FOMC decides to change policy, it typically does so via nuances—some subtle, some not so subtle—in how it adds or drains reserves. To get a better flavor as to how open market operations are utilized to transmit or to put into effect a policy change, we will review two operating procedures. One is a federal funds targeting approach, as is currently being employed under Chairman Greenspan. The other is a reserves or borrowings strategy that was utilized prior to the currently favored tactics. By analyzing these two methods, one will have a broad base from which to analyze any future type of operating mechanism that the Fed may choose to employ.

A Federal Funds Targeting Approach

In many ways, utilization of this approach makes life a lot easier for market analysts. For the most part, it is much more effortless to read a Fed policy change when the Fed is targeting the federal funds rate than when it is using just about any other type of operating procedure.

To begin with, it is important to remember that the federal funds rate is the only market rate over which the Fed has some degree of control. This is because it is the rate that banks pay for reserves. Since the Fed has a significant say about the supply/demand balance of reserves at any given point in time, it has a major influence on what the price of those reserves will be. Furthermore, under this approach the Fed designates the federal funds rate around which trading occurs.

Without going into a major digression about the federal funds market[3] it will suffice to say that beyond the Fed's ability to

---

3   For a fuller discussion of the federal funds market, see Stigm, Marcia, *The Money Market*, 3rd Ed., Homewood, IL, Richard Irwin, 1992, pp. 537–574.

arbitrarily change the federal funds rate, there is a technical relationship that determines where the federal funds rate trades relative to the discount rate and a market effect that contributes to the where federal funds trade relative to where the Fed would like it to trade. The former link will be explored when we cover the borrowings approach to open market operations. For the current discussion, it is the market's resolution of the federal funds rate that matters most.

Day to day, or even week to week, factors outside of the Fed's control can affect where federal funds trade. Banks may be less willing to lend their surplus of reserves, banks may want to hold a greater amount of excess reserves, or maybe the system just isn't efficiently distributing the reserves from the "haves" to the "have nots." But these gyrations will typically occur around an equilibrium federal funds rate established by the Federal Reserve, when the Fed is operating under a federal funds targeting approach. When the reserve flows return to normal, the federal funds rate will return to (at least within five or so basis points) the rate deigned by the Fed to be the equilibrium. The Fed establishes this rate by sending signals to the marketplace that it would like to see the federal funds rate lower or higher and then sending additional signals as to how much higher or lower the federal funds rate should move. It does this via open market operations.

An Example

To show how the Fed transmits its policy changes under a federal funds rate targeting approach, let's assume that the Fed works through its reserve numbers and projects an add need for the upcoming maintenance period of $2 bn. that is evenly distributed throughout the two weeks. Assuming that market analysts come up with a similar projection, market participants would be expecting the Fed to conduct a $2 bn. round of customers in its normal intervention time, 11:30 a.m. to 11:35 a.m., every day of the reserve period. And if policy were status quo, that is what the Fed would do. But let us further assume that for one of the reasons discussed in the last chapter, the FOMC decides to ease policy. When the decision is made, it is up to open market operations to transmit that change to the marketplace. Within this framework we can distinguish between three types of policy signals.

1. The federal funds rate level. Under the federal funds rate-targeting approach, the federal funds rate level at which the Fed conducts its operations is usually deemed the most critical interpretive element. For any given policy stance, there is a targeted federal funds rate. Movement will occur around that rate, depending upon technical market conditions, but in general the market will come to associate a particular federal funds rate level with a particular Fed policy stance. Under the federal funds targeting approach, it is particularly important to watch at what federal funds rate level open market operations are conducted. Thus, if the presumed equilibrium rate for funds is 3 percent, the Fed typically would add reserves only when funds were trading at or over 3 percent. Even within this context, if funds were trading right at 3 percent, customer repos would more than likely be the extent of a reserve addition, under relatively normal reserve conditions. The markets, in this instance, would assume system repos would be conducted only when funds were trading above 3 percent, say at 3 1/16 percent or higher. Likewise, matched sales would be conducted only when funds were trading below 3 percent.

To announce a policy change, the Fed could conduct an operation when funds were trading outside of the band normally associated with that action. If the equilibrium funds rate was 3 percent, and the Fed conducted system repos at 3 percent, there would be a strong inference that the Fed wished to see the federal funds rate lower. Conducting customer repos, and certainly conducting system repos, with funds below the perceived equilibrium federal funds rate would send an even clearer signal. In the same vein, an easing could be transmitted by not draining reserves with funds below the accepted Fed target, in this example at 2 7/8 percent. This level would normally be assumed to warrant a round of matched sales. In each instance, it could be inferred that the Fed desired the federal funds rate to drop. On the tightening side, conducting matched sales at 3 percent or higher would convey a strong sense that the Fed wished to see the federal funds rate higher. Or the Fed could defer adding reserves when the federal funds rate was (again in this example) at 3 1/8 percent.

2. Type or size of open market operation. In the previous instance in which an easing move was mandated by the FOMC, the Fed could conduct an open market operation, that added, or at least looked to add, more reserves than was necessary. In the previous example, a $3 bn. customer repo technically would do the trick of adding more reserves than were needed or expected. But an overnight system repo would be the clearest signal that a change was in the offing. This is especially true if the federal funds were trading at or very near the perceived target rate. The reason is that a $3 bn. customer, while adding more reserves, could easily be overlooked as a policy signal. This is because reserve projections by private analysts and the Fed are subject to sizeable error, and a $3 bn. customer instead of a $2 bn. customer is well within the normal forecast error range. That is why a system repo in this instance would be the preferred choice of the Fed, especially since under a federal funds targeting approach the Federal Reserve typically does not try to disguise its policy changes. In fact, one could almost term this procedure an announcement approach. For it is the announcement of a system repo at a time that it was not necessary that sends the signal, not the exact size of the operation. Remember, the market does not know the size of a system repo immediately. And often, once the size of the system is revealed subsequently, it is found to be no bigger than a customer repo. Nevertheless, by conducting an operation that seemingly is more aggressive than is expected or necessary, the Federal Reserve sends the signal that it wants the federal funds rate to drop.

This announcement's effect, via the choice of operations, can employ the full spectrum of open market instruments. For easing, the Fed could conduct a customer repo when no adding was necessary. Just as possible is not an actual adding of reserves but a situation in which the Fed does not conduct matched sales when reserves were in excess supply. This is as overt a policy signal as announcing a larger addition of reserves than was thought necessary. When tightening, the Federal Reserve could conduct overnight matched sales when no intervention was required or when term matched sales looked to be appropriate. Or it could conduct a customer repo when a system

FIGURE 27–1 Changes in Fed Policy Via Open Market Operations: 1989–1992

Date	Action	Federal Funds Rate Effect
Jan. 1, 1989	$1.5 bn. CRP	Fed raises rate 25 b.p.
June 6, 1989	No action with Fed funds below equilibrium	Fed lowers rate 25 b.p.
July 6, 1989	No action with Fed funds below equilibrium	Fed lowers rate 25 b.p.
July 25, 1989	No action with Fed funds below equilibrium	Fed lowers rate 25 b.p.
Oct. 16, 1989	$2.5 bn. CRP	Fed lowers rate 25 b.p.
Nov. 6, 1989	$2.5 bn. CRP	Fed lowers rate 25 b.p.
Dec. 20, 1989	Overnight SRP	Fed lowers rate 25 b.p.
July 13, 1990	Overnight SRP	Fed lowers rate 25 b.p.
Oct. 29, 1990	$1 bn. CRP	Fed lowers rate 25 b.p.
Nov. 16, 1990	Overnight SRP	Fed lowers rate 25 b.p.
Dec. 7, 1990	$1.5 bn. CRP	Fed lowers rate 25 b.p.
Jan. 8, 1991	No action with Fed funds below equilibrium	
Feb. 2, 1991	Overnight SRP	Fed lowers rate 25 b.p.
Aug. 6, 1991	Overnight SRP	Fed lowers rate 25 b.p.
Oct. 29, 1991	No action with Fed funds below equilibrium	Fed lowers rate 25 b.p.
Dec. 6, 1991	$3 bn. CRP	Fed lowers rate 25 b.p.
April 9, 1992	Overnight SRP	Fed lowers rate 25 b.p.
Sept. 4, 1992	$2.5 bn. CRP	Fed lowers rate 25 b.p.

Eighteen policy signals: 6 overnight system repos, 7 customer repos, and 5 no action.
b.p. = basis points

repo was expected and necessary. A commonly accepted view is that overnight systems are the chief vehicle for announcing an ease. But, in fact, customer repos were used more frequently to signal an ease in the 1989 through 1992 period than were overnight system repos; indeed, no intervention was used as a policy signal a fair portion of the time as well. (See Figure 27–1.) The one operation that usually has no policy implications is the term operation, either system repos or matched sales. Each is considered strictly technical by the market, and the Fed treats them as such also.

3. Timing of the operation. As already discussed, the Fed usually times its open market operations to coincide with the reserve movement it is offsetting. However, in an effort to signal a policy change it can mistime its operations. It can add or drain reserves before or after the interval in which it otherwise would have conducted the operations if policy remained unchanged. For instance, if there were a $4 bn. add need in the second half of a maintenance period, an unchanged policy stance would dictate systems in the final seven days. But to announce a policy change, the Fed could begin adding the reserves via system repos in the first week of the period. Similarly, it could delay draining reserves to signal an ease. In an effort to push interest rates higher, The Federal Reserve could drain before it was necessary or delay adding reserves until well after a reserve shortage had developed.

Is It a Policy Move or a Technical Operation?

In some circumstances a move by the Fed to inject reserves or drain reserves can seem an unambiguous move to change the federal funds rate target. But one thing that should be made clear is that this clarity of purpose is not always in evidence. Sometimes when an initial signal is sent, it is not understood, and sometimes the market thinks it sees a signal when there is none. Again, the Fed does not explicitly announce a change in the federal funds rate the way it announces a discount rate change; it sends a message it figures the market will understand. But there are ambiguities to reading the Fed's intentions: there are numerous examples of the marketplace improperly reading the Fed's signals. The chief reason is that the federal funds rate for reasons already mentioned can deviate from the targeted rate for days at a time without reflecting Federal Reserve policy changes. These deviations can compromise the Fed's ability to meet a technical reserve need and force it to conduct open market operations (or not conduct them) at levels that might be associated with a policy change. Remember, the Fed ultimately tries to ensure an equilibrium in the reserve market at the targeted funds rate, so it may have to forge ahead with open market operations regardless of where federal funds are trading so as not to be confronted with a very large disequilibrium in the reserve market later in the period. It is especially under these circumstances that the Fed's intentions can be misread.

The degree to which open market operations are restricted by the federal funds rate also can depend on the economic background. If the economic data offer absolutely no reason to expect the Fed to change policy, the Fed might inject reserves with funds slightly below target if an add need exists and it feels not doing so would push funds too high later in the reserve period. But the Fed probably wouldn't take such a course if the economic data hinted that an easing might be necessary. This would mislead the market. Another culprit to misunderstood intentions is the marketplace itself. In certain circumstances, the market will sometimes "test the Fed." For instance, assume the reserve position was projected by the Fed as a small add need (a shortage of reserves). But also assume that due to economic circumstances the market thinks that the Fed might ease. Even with a small add need the market could trade federal funds rate at 2 7/8 percent (if the target were 3 percent). Faced with no need to drain reserves, the Fed would have to decide whether to protest the low funds rate by conducting a matched sale operation or simply adhere to the technical reserve picture (do nothing) and let the market find out the hard way that no policy change is under way. In this instance, an actual draining operation would send a clear signal to the market and then the Fed could go about its technical reserve business. But by initially not draining with funds below the perceived target, some in the marketplace could misinterpret the Fed's intentions. Those intentions ultimately would become apparent, though, as the reserve shortage built and the federal funds rate ultimately rose sharply. In the interim, though, there could be widespread disagreement as to what the Fed was up to.

This potential ambiguity in Federal Reserve operations just emphasizes the point that "Fed-watching" is an art, not a science. It requires a constant reading of the Fed, how it has behaved in the past, and how that behavior changes as the economic landscape changes. Only then will one have a solid chance at properly interpreting Fed reserve actions.

A Borrowings Target Approach

The nitty-gritty details of open market operations are not critically important under a federal funds operating approach. As we have seen, Fed policy changes are not associated with technical changes in any specific reserve factors. A feel for where federal funds should trade and what action the Fed is projected to conduct is generically sufficient to interpret Fed policy signals. Of course, one has to be able to come up with a reserve projection before one can ascertain whether or not a given open market operation was different than what was technically necessary.

But the Fed has not always employed this operating strategy, and there is no reason to believe it will continue to use it in the years ahead. As the economic situation and the composition of the Federal Reserve changes, the Fed's operating procedures can change as well.

Taking some liberties, the alternatives can be grouped together under the heading of reserves targeting approaches, with the one most recently employed in the mid-to-late 1980s being the borrowings target approach. A look at this less overt, more technical method of changing policy provides a most interesting contrast to federal funds targeting and brings the number-crunching aspect of reserve forecasting to the forefront. It also shows that as obscure and somewhat enigmatic as the federal funds approach may be, reserves targeting is even more so, and it requires an even precise knowledge of the Fed's balance sheet and its operating procedures.

The Technical Aspects of a Borrowings Approach

A discussion of the borrowings target approach necessitates bringing back the T-accounts and conveying two very important and related points. The first is, under the borrowings target approach, that it is assumed that *the level of borrowed reserves directly affects the spread between the federal funds rate and the discount rate.*

Thus, an increase (decrease) in the level of borrowed reserves increases (decreases) the spread. But the level of borrowings does not set the *level* of the federal funds rate. One can have borrowed reserves at $200 mn. and have a 3 percent funds rate or a 10 percent funds rate.

The second is a more fundamental issue regarding how banks meet their reserve need. In general, banks are reluctant to borrow from their district Federal Reserve banks. Some do so for seasonal reasons, but one should assume that banks first go into the federal funds market to purchase nonborrowed reserves to meet their reserve needs. If a bank is caught short of reserves at the end of the maintenance period, it will go to its district Federal Reserve bank, but there is a stigma attached to borrowing frequently from the discount window, and just as importantly the Federal Reserve discourages frequent use of the window. In both senses, it is safe to consider the discount window as residual supplier of reserves to the banking system.

This latter point is the key to the Fed's policy changes under a borrowings approach. If the Fed changes the borrowings level, it should be able to alter the federal funds rate. To see how this works, let us bring back the reserve factor changes used under the technical section.

Reserves

Increase Supply		Decrease Supply	
Decrease Demand		Increase Demand	
Float	1000	Required Reserves	2000
		Excess Reserves	500
		Treasury Balance at Fed	1000
		Currency in Circulation	500
Sum:	1000		4000

These changes resulted in an add need of $3 bn. But as one can see, there was no change in borrowed reserves. Now let's assume that for macroeconomic reasons, growth is very strong and inflation is picking up, the FOMC decides to tighten policy. We will assume that the reserve period began with the FOMC having targeted borrowings at $500 mn. This level of borrowings is associated with an unchanged policy that is with the federal funds rate trading a certain number of basis points above the discount rate. Under a decree to tighten policy, the FOMC decides to increase the level of borrowings to $1.5 bn. The result is the following T-account:

Reserves

Increase Supply		Decrease Supply	
Decrease Demand		Increase Demand	
Float	1000	Required Reserves	2000
Borrowed Reserves	1000	Excess Reserves	500
		Treasury Balance at Fed	1000
		Currency in Circulation	500
	2000		4000

Now, how does this increase the spread of the federal funds rate over the discount rate? Remember that banks initially go to the federal funds market to meet their reserve needs. By increasing the borrowings target, the Fed is shifting the composition of the supply of reserves. Thus, when banks go into the federal funds market they essentially will find that the nonborrowed reserves are undersupplied by $1 bn. With demand greater than supply, the federal funds rate will move higher. Banks ultimately will be forced to go to the discount window for the $1 bn. in reserves; but because they tried to avoid doing so initially, the federal funds rate is pushed higher. This effectively "tightens policy." One can also see that one important difference between this operating procedure and the federal funds targeting approach is that the federal funds rate is subject to much more volatility and uncertainty under the borrowings target approach.

For anyone watching the Fed in search of clues to policy changes, the key is that the add need, *for the Fed*, now is only $2 bn. Market participants and analysts, however, not knowing the Fed has changed policy, still have borrowings at $500 mn. and a need to add $3 bn. in reserves. Thus, when the time comes for the Fed to intervene, the market will be expecting systems or a large $3 bn. customer. When the Fed comes in and adds only $2 bn., that will signal that it is supplying fewer reserves and is tightening policy. But instead of signaling a policy change with one reserve operation that is overtly different from what was called for, the operation this time around is only marginally different than expected. Remember that under a federal funds targeting approach such a slight difference was viewed as probably being a forecast miss and not a policy change. In this instance, though, the Fed will continue to undersupply reserves, continually conducting $2 bn. customer repos.

The big difference for the market is that the Fed no longer offers up the one-time announcement associated with the federal funds targeting approach. Now the market does not have the luxury of being hit over the head with a policy change; it must understand to a much greater degree the nuances of open market operations.

The Borrowings Approach: Some General Guidelines

The three ways in which one analyzes Fed operations under a funds targeting approach (i.e., the type of operation, the timing of an operation, and the level at which funds are trading when an operation is conducted) are just as interpretively critical under a borrowings approach. But where these are enough to discern a change in policy under a funds targeting approach, one often must go beyond these signals to discern a change under a borrowings target approach.

1. Look at the actual borrowings number. On the weekly H4.1 balance sheet for the Federal Reserve System, the Fed reports its "Loans to depository institutions," or in plain jargon, bank borrowings from the discount window. This is what the Fed actually is targeting, and it seemingly would be the ultimate clue to a change in policy. Unfortunately, things are not so easy, since the relationship between the borrowings level and the federal funds rate is unstable. First, the previous example exaggerated the change in borrowings that occurs when policy changes. Changes in the borrowing's target typically run in $50 mn. increments. That, in theory, still should be noticeable. However, the Fed is almost never able to hit its target right on the nose. For many different reasons, borrowings will run higher or lower than the target by margins often exceeding $100 mn. The noise inherent in the borrowings data makes it a less than perfect indicator of a policy change under this approach. Often, it could take two or three weeks of borrowings data to determine whether or not the Fed has changed policy.

2. Estimates of reserve factor changes are subject to significant error. It would be nice if market estimates of the reserve need were extremely accurate. But analysts are dealing with a limited amount of information in projecting reserve needs and can miss substantially. In fact, the Fed misses, too. In 1992, its average miss on the first day of a new maintenance period for period average reserve factors (not including required or excess reserves) was a little over $1 bn. This miss dropped to about $425 mn. in mid-period and only about $75 mn. on the final day of the statement period. But these errors are compounded for private analysts, who have much less day-to-day information with which to work. Under such circumstances, one can see that deciding whether a reserve action only slightly different than expected is a policy change is very difficult. Add to this the fact previously mentioned, that borrowings target changes are in small increments, and it becomes clear that one may be faced with deciding whether or not a $700 mn. customer repo instead of a $1.0 bn. customer is a policy move, knowing full well how large one's margin of error can be.

3. The Fed's choice: speak softly or carry a big stick. Under a borrowings target approach the Fed has greater latitude in deciding how to advertise its policy change. Sometimes, to get its change in policy across clearly, it will flagrantly signal the policy change by, for example, conducting operations at a funds level clearly out of line with equilibrium. This is akin to the signals sent via a federal funds targeting approach. Other times it can choose to be a bit more obscure and just under- or oversupply reserves by a modest amount. In the past, it has taken weeks for the market to decide whether or not the Fed has changed policy. It all depends upon how much public attention the Fed wants to draw to its actions.

One final overall point. Regardless of the type of operating procedure, the Fed is not intent upon creating an imbalance of reserves within the system. Certainly if at a given point in time the funds rate is stubbornly high or low, the Fed may be overly generous or stingy with its supply of reserves in order to help bring the federal funds rate back to target. But these are the exceptions, not the rule. The phrases sometimes heard, such as "the Fed isn't pumping enough liquidity into the system," or "the Fed should be taking liquidity out of the system," are not pertinent to open market operations. The Fed supplies or withdraws reserves in order to keep the supply and demand in balance. Its open market operations and changes in policy are conducted within this framework.

Remembering this point provides a useful backdrop for analyzing and understanding the Federal Reserve's daily activities. Not many will want to become involved in computing reserve forecasts, but anyone interested in the direction of interest rates should have a basic understanding of how the Fed operates. Customer repos, system repos, and matched sales are the Federal Reserve's most frequently employed policy instruments. And given that the Federal Reserve is the prime generator of short-term interest rate changes, understanding its actions is fundamental to knowing where interest rates are headed.

Changes in Policy Using the Discount Rate

As mentioned in the previous chapter, discount rate changes are made by the Federal Reserve Board. In fact, the board has to act upon a request from one of the 12 Federal Reserve Districts in order to change the rate (not that a request cannot be made to order, but one is necessary). Once a request is made, the board, after the appropriate discussions, votes on the matter and officially announces the change. The actual statement is greeted with great interest by financial markets. Just as FOMC minutes are scrutinized for clues to Fed policy signals, so are the statements accompanying discount rate changes. Usually, they detail the reasons for the change, providing some insight into the Federal Reserve Board's current policy focus. For example, following are the key sections of the Federal Reserve Board's announcement accompanying the discount rate change on September 13, 1991:

"The Federal Reserve Board announced on September 13, 1991 a reduction in the discount rate from 5.5% to 5%, effective immediately.

"Action was taken in light of weakness in the money and credit aggregates, the improving inflation environment, and concerns about the ongoing strength of the economic expansion.

The reduction, in part, realigns the discount rate with market interest rates."

In this instance, it was important to note two things: (1) the three reasons cited for the discount rate change and (2) the fact that money and credit growth were first on the list of reasons for the change. That ranking made their behavior key variables to watch in the future.

The use of a discount rate change instead of a federal funds rate change typically infers a more aggressive Fed policy stance. Since 1982 all but one discount rate change has been for 50 basis points. The exception was a 100-basis point change announced on December 20, 1991. Changes in policy via the federal funds rate, however, typically are worth 25 basis points.

The aggressive nature of a discount rate change has meant the Federal Reserve typically employs it as a policy tool when a strong statement about its policy actions is necessary and/or when economic conditions warrant an assertive move. One technical instance in which the Federal Reserve would choose a discount rate cut regardless of the intent of its policy change is when the federal funds rate is trading at the discount rate. Since according to current Federal Reserve procedures the discount rate is not a penalty rate, it will be set at or under the federal funds rate. Thus, the Fed has little choice but to use a discount rate cut if it wants to lower rates when the federal funds target rate is at the discount rate. There is no problem, however, if the Fed wants to raise the discount rate at a time the rate is the same as the federal funds rate target. The federal funds rate will follow the discount rate higher, immediately following the Fed's policy action.

Once the discount rate has been changed, the Fed must define where it wants the federal funds rate to trade relative to the new discount rate. It does so via open market operations. Immediately following a discount rate change, the market will move the funds rate to the level it thinks is the new target rate. The Fed, during the subsequent intervention time, can ratify the market's perception, usually by conducting a customer repo or not intervening at all, or it can tell the market it is targeting a different level by more aggressively conducting a matched sale or overnight system repo.

References

Madigan, Brian F., and Warren T. Trepeta, "Implementation of Monetary Policy," In *Changes in Money Market Instruments and Procedures: Objectives and Implications*, Bank for International Settlements, March 1986.

Meek, Paul, "Open Market Operations," Federal Reserve Bank of New York, ed. of 1963, 1969, 1973, 1978, and 1985.

Meek, Paul, *U.S. Monetary Policy and Financial Markets*, Federal Reserve Bank of New York, October 1982.

Meulendyke, Ann-Marie, "A Review of Federal Reserve Policy Targets and Operating Guides in Recent Decades." Federal Reserve Bank of New York Monthly Review, Autumn 1988, 6–17.

Chapter 28

Treasury Financing

General Description

The U.S. Treasury's financing schedule has evolved slowly over time. The changes are infrequent; they're measured in years rather than in months or quarters. For example, the most recent change occurred in May 1993. Then the extremely positive shape of the yield curve caused the Treasury to attempt to cut its borrowing costs by financing more debt with shorter maturities and less with longer maturities. It did so by announcing the elimination of the seven-year notes, reducing the total annual size and frequency of 30-year bonds, and by announcing that it would be raising the size of its shorter offerings—weekly bills, year bills, two-year notes, and three-year notes. This had been the first change in the financing schedule since December 1990. Then the Treasury eliminated the once a quarter four-year note from the financing cycle and moved to a monthly five-year note auction, instead of its previous once-a-quarter frequency.

These intermittent changes conform to the U.S. Treasury's stated preference for creating as little uncertainty as possible in meeting its new cash needs. In this respect, changes have come about as the Treasury has been forced to accommodate the ever burgeoning deficit or to find ways to cut rising interest expenses rather than through a desire simply to tinker with its financing pattern.

The Financing Schedule

The nature of the calendar makes it impossible to ensure specific auction and settlement dates from month to month or year to year. If a specific settlement date falls on a weekend, the actual transaction will take place on the following business day. For example, two- and five-year notes always mature on the last day of the month, which, if that date falls on a weekend, means the actual settlement takes place on the first business day of the following month. A settlement scheduled for a holiday would also be pushed forward to the next business day of the following month. A settlement scheduled for a holidays would also be pushed forward to the next business day. Similarly, the auctions of the three-year note, ten-year note, and semiannual 30-year bonds settle on the fifteenth of the month. If that date is on a weekend, they will settle on the first business day after the weekend. This fact actually can change the dates on which the three securities are auctioned. If there is a post-weekend settle-

FIGURE 28–1 U.S. Treasury's Financing Pattern

Security	Frequency	Announced	Auctioned	Settlement
Three-month bill	Weekly	Tues	Mon	Thurs
Six-month bill	Weekly	Tues	Mon	Thurs
One-year bill	Every four weeks	Friday	Thursday	Thurs
Two-year note	Monthly	Typically 3rd Wed	Typically last or next to last Tues	Last day of month
Three-year note	Quarterly: Feb, May, Aug, Nov	First Wed of auction month	Tuesday following auction announcement	The 15th of auction month
Five-year notes	Monthly	Typically 3rd Wed of the month	Typically last or next to last Wed of month	Last day of month
10-year notes	Quarterly: Feb, May, Aug, Nov	First Wed of the month	Wed following auction announcement	The 15th of auction month
30-year bonds	Semi-annually: Feb, May	First Wed of the month	Thurs following auction announcement	The 15th of auction month

ment, the refunding auctions will be pushed back one week. (See Figure 28–1.)

The quarterly auctioning of the three- and 10-year issues and the semiannual auction of the 30-year bonds is commonly referred to as the "refunding." The auctions come (again, typically) three days in succession and are timed to settle on the day of the Treasury's quarterly interest payments on its outstanding debt. This interest payment outflow has assumed massive proportions and requires a sizeable inflow of new cash as an offset. For fixed-income participants the refundings are the recurring mountain the Treasury market constantly has to scale, and how well the three auctions go is often considered a sign of the fixed-income market's health.

Cash Management Bills

Another means of financing that the Treasury employs is the issuance of cash management bills. Historically, their purpose was to tide the Treasury over temporary cash low points, typically the weeks prior to tax dates. But the length and size of these bills also has evolved to meet the Treasury's increasing needs for more money. As previously stated, these bills usually had maturities of just a few weeks and typically not more than 30 days. But as cash requirements have increased, the Treasury has utilized these bills to bring in money for longer periods of time. Whereas cash management bills had always matured within the same quarter, the deficits of the 1980s forced the Treasury to extend the maturity of some bills to the point where they bridged quarters, culminating in some issues crossing fiscal years and having maturities of close to one year.

Unlike the set schedule for the Treasury's bills, notes, and bonds, the size and timing of the issuance of cash management bills is subject to great variability. The volatility and uncertainty of the U.S. Treasury's cash position makes it impossible to have any strict regularity in cash management bill issuance. But that having been said, there are seasonal periods that are more susceptible to cash low points. The schedule below indicates when these bills typically have been issued in the past and stand a good chance of being issued in the future. In any specific year,

FIGURE 28–2 Cash Management Bills

Issuance	Possible Maturity
Mid-March to early April	2nd half of April (post-April 15)
Late May to early June	Late June
Mid-to-late August	2nd half of Sept/Late Jan/Late April
Mid-November	Late Dec/Late Jan/Late April
Early December	Late Dec (post-Dec 15)

the Treasury could issue bills at any, all, or none of the times listed in Figure 28–2.

Auction Sizes

In general, the sizes of the auctions are inversely related to maturity: the largest issues have a maturity of one year or less. The weekly auction of the three- and six-month bills (which are scheduled on 13- and 26-week maturity cycles) are usually announced in one combined size. Thus, an announced $24 bn. weekly bill auction implies the 13-week bill is for $12 bn. and the 26-week bill is for $12 bn. It isn't unusual for the year bill (auctioned on a 52-week cycle) to be of greater size than the weekly bills, individually, however. Further exceptions to the "longer the maturity the smaller the size" guidelines are usually due to differing frequency of issuance. Thus, the three-year note can be larger than the two-year note because it is auctioned only quarterly compared to the two-year note's monthly frequency. Similarly, the 30-year bonds semiannual auction schedule necessitates its larger size.

Given that the Treasury's needs can vary quarter to quarter, the Treasury has to be flexible with its financing needs. As already mentioned, cash management bills serve such a purpose. In addition, the Treasury will alter (sometimes sharply) the size of its weekly bill auctions, as another means of regulating its cashflow (see Figure 28–3). Typically, this will happen in the second calendar quarter when the Treasury's financing needs are their lowest due to strong tax receipts. Drops of $1 bn. to $2 bn. from one week to the next in bill auction volumes are not uncommon, but they are typically reversed as the July-September quarter begins. The Treasury also will cut back on the size of

FIGURE 28–3 Snapshot: Auction Sizes May 1993

Three-and six-month bills	$23.2 bn. (week of 5/10/93)
One-year bill	$14.25 bn.
Two-year note	$15.5 bn
Three-year note	$16 bn.
Five-year note	$11 bn.
10-year note	$10.75 bn.
30-year bond	$8.25 bn. (before the switch to semi-annual auctions)

its coupon auctions, usually by a more modest $250 mn or $500 mn. if it finds itself in a particularly comfortable cash position for more than just a few weeks.

The Treasury's announcement of its auction sizes presently are made at 2:30 p.m. The exception is the quarterly refunding, which is announced at 2:45 p.m. At the refunding announcement, the Treasury also releases the schedule of auction dates up until the next refunding. On the Mondays immediately before the quarterly refunding announcements at 3:00 p.m., the Treasury releases its own estimates of its financing needs for the remainder of the current quarter and for the following quarter. Such estimates are useful for gauging the size of upcoming auction amounts for bills and coupons. Analysts can compare their own estimates with those of the Treasury, knowing full well that the actual amounts of new cash raised, especially in the subsequent quarter, can vary significantly from their own and the Treasury's estimates.

Appendices

Appendix 1

U.S. Business Cycle Turning Point Dates

U.S. Business Cycle Turning Point Dates

Peak	Trough
November 1948	October 1949
July 1953	May 1954
August 1957	April 1958
April 1960	February 1961
December 1969	November 1970
November 1973	March 1975
January 1980	July 1980
July 1981	November 1982
July 1990	March 1991

Source: National Bureau of Economic Research and the U.S. Department of Commerce.

Appendix 2

Consumer Inflation Cycle

Consumer Inflation Cycle Turning Point Dates

Peak	Trough
November 1946	July 1949
February 1951	March 1959
August 1953	October 1954
March 1958	May 1959
October 1959	June 1961
October 1966	May 1967
April 1970	August 1972
September 1974	April 1976
March 1980	March 1983
February 1984	April 1986
October 1990	September 1992^T

T = Tentative

Appendix 3

Commodity Prices Indexes

Commodity Research Bureau (CRB) Futures Index
(21 commodities averaged over 9 months, equal weights)

Industrial	Food, Grain, Other	Speculative
Copper	Cattle	Gold
Lumber	Cocoa	Platinum
Crude Oil	Coffee	Silver
Heating Oil	Corn	
Cotton	Hogs	
	Pork Bellies	
	Oats	
	Orange Juice	
	Soybeans	
	Soybean Meal	
	Soybean Oil	
	Sugar	
	Wheat (Chicago)	

Commodity Research Bureau (CRB) Spot Index
(31 commodities, equal weights)

Industrial	Food, Grain, Other	Speculative
Copper Scrap	Butter	
Hides	Cocoa	
Lead	Corn	
Print Cloth	Hogs	
Rosin	Lard	
Rubber	Soybean Oil	
Steel Scrap	Steers	
Tin	Sugar	
Wool Tops	Wheat (Minneapolis)	
Cotton	Wheat (Kansas City)	
Tallow		
Burlap		
Zinc		

Journal of Commerce (JOC) Spot Index
(18 commodities, Weights as shown)

Industrial		Food, Grain, Other	Speculative
Cotton (5.9%)	Textiles (17.4%)		
Burlap (5.5%)			
Polyester (2.7%)			
Print Cloth (3.3%)			
Steel Scrap (6.3%)	Metals (34.5%)		
Copper Scrap (6.6%)			
Aluminum (6.1%)			
Zinc (5.1%)			
Lead (5.1%)			
Tin (5.0%)			
Hides (5.5%)	Miscellaneous (48.0%)		
Rubber (6.3%)			
Tallow (5.2%)			
Plywood (7.9%)			
Corrugated Boxes (6.3%)			
Red Oak (5.0%)			
Benzene (4.7%)			
Crude Oil (7.1%)			

Appendix 4

Prime Rate History

	PRIME RATE HISTORY--JAN 11, 1983 TO PRESENT	SOURCE: FRB H.15			
DATE	RATE	DATE	RATE	DATE	RATE
07/02/92 -PRESENT	6.00	05/11/88-07/14/88	9.00	01/15/85-05/17/85	10.50
12/23/91-07/01/92	6.50	02/02/88-05/10/88	8.50	12/20/84-01/16/85	10.75
11/06/91-12/20/91	7.50	11/05/87-02/01/88	8.75	11/28/84-12/19/84	11.25
09/13/91-11/06/91	8.00	10/22/87-11/04/87	9.00	11/09/84-11/27/84	11.75
05/01/91-09/12/91	8.50	10/07/87-10/21/87	9.25	10/29/84-11/08/84	12.00
02/01/91-05/01/91	9.00	09/04/87-10/06/87	8.75	10/17/84-10/28/84	12.50
01/02/91-02/01/91	9.50	05/15/87-09/03/87	8.25	09/27/84-10/16/84	12.75
01/08/90-01/02/91	10.00	05/01/87-05/14/87	8.00	06/25/84-09/26/84	13.00
07/31/89-01/07/90	10.50	04/01/87-04/30/87	7.75	05/08/84-06/24/84	12.50
06/05/89-07/28/89	11.00	08/26/86-03/31/87	7.50	04/05/84-05/07/84	12.00
02/24/89-06/03/89	11.50	07/11/86-08/25/86	8.00	03/19/84-04/04/84	11.50
02/10/89-02/23/89	11.00	04/21/86-07/10/86	8.50	08/08/83-03/18/84	11.00
11/28/88-02/09/89	10.50	03/07/86-04/20/86	9.00	02/28/83-08/05/83	10.50
08/11/88-11/27/88	10.00	06/18/85-03/06/86	9.50	01/11/83-02/25/83	11.00
07/14/88-08/10/88	9.50	05/20/85-06/17/85	10.00		

	PRIME RATE HISTORY--NOV 26, 1980 TO JAN 10, 1983	SOURCE: FRB NY			
DATE	RATE	DATE	RATE	DATE	RATE
11/22/82-01/10/83	11.50	11/17/81-11/19/81	17.00	04/24/81-04/29/81	17.50
10/14/82-11/21/82	12.00	11/17/81-11/17/81	16.50	04/02/81-04/23/81	17.00
10/07/82-11/13/82	13.00	11/09/81-11/16/81	17.00	03/17/81-04/01/81	17.50
08/23/82-10/06/82	13.50	11/03/81-11/08/81	17.50	03/10/81-03/16/81	18.00
08/18/82-08/22/82	14.00	10/13/81-11/02/81	18.00	02/23/81-03/09/81	19.00
08/16/82-08/17/82	14.50	10/05/81-10/12/81	19.00	02/03/81-02/22/81	19.50
08/02/82-08/15/82	15.00	09/22/81-10/02/81	19.50	01/09/81-02/02/81	20.00
07/29/82-08/01/82	15.50	09/15/81-09/21/81	20.00	01/02/81-01/08/81	20.50
07/20/82-08/28/82	16.00	07/08/81-09/14/81	20.50	12/19/80-01/01/81	21.50
02/23/82-07/19/82	16.50	06/03/81-07/07/81	20.00	12/16/80-12/18/80	21.00
02/18/82-02/22/82	17.00	05/22/81-06/02/81	20.50	12/10/80-12/15/80	20.00
02/02/82-02/17/82	16.50	05/19/81-05/21/81	20.00	12/05/80-12/09/80	19.00
12/01/81-02/01/82	15.75	05/11/81-05/18/81	19.50	12/02/80-12/04/80	18.50
11/24/81-11/30/81	16.00	05/04/81-05/10/81	19.00	11/26/80-12/01/80	17.75
11/20/81-11/23/81	16.50	04/30/81-05/03/81	18.00		

	PRIME RATE HISTORY--SEP 07, 1979 TO NOV 25, 1980	SOURCE: FRB-NY			
DATE	RATE	DATE	RATE	DATE	RATE
11/21/80-11/25/80	17.00	06/13/80-06/19/80	12.50	03/04/80-03/06/80	17.25
11/17/80-11/20/80	16.25	06/06/80-06/12/80	13.00	02/29/80-03/03/80	16.75
11/06/80-11/16/80	15.50	05/30/80-06/05/80	14.00	02/22/80-02/28/80	16.25
10/29/80-11/05/80	14.50	05/23/80-05/29/80	14.50	02/19/80-02/21/80	15.75
10/17/80-10/28/80	14.00	05/16/80-05/22/80	16.50	12/07/79-02/18/80	15.25
10/01/80-10/16/80	13.50	05/07/80-05/15/80	17.50	11/30/79-12/06/79	15.50
09/26/80-09/30/80	13.00	05/02/80-05/06/80	18.50	11/16/79-11/29/79	15.75
09/19/80-09/25/80	12.50	05/01/80-05/01/80	19.00	11/09/79-11/15/79	15.50
09/12/80-09/18/80	12.25	05/01/80-05/01/80	18.50	11/01/79-11/08/79	15.25
09/08/80-09/11/80	12.00	04/18/80-04/30/80	19.50	10/23/79-10/31/79	15.00
08/27/80-09/07/80	11.50	04/02/80-04/17/80	20.00	10/09/79-10/22/79	14.50
08/22/80-08/26/80	11.25	03/28/80-04/01/80	19.50	09/28/79-10/08/79	13.50
07/25/80-08/21/80	11.00	03/19/80-03/27/80	19.00	09/21/79-09/27/79	13.25
07/07/80-07/24/80	11.50	03/14/80-03/18/80	18.50	09/14/79-09/20/79	13.00
06/20/80-07/06/80	12.00	03/07/80-03/13/80	17.75	09/07/79-09/13/79	12.75

Appendix 5

Discount Rate History

DISCOUNT RATE HISTORY--AUG 31, 1977 TO PRESENT SOURCE: FRB-NY						
DATE (BY WEEK)	RATE	DATE (BY WEEK)	RATE	DATE (BY WEEK)	RATE
07/02/92- PRESENT	3.00	12/24/84-05/17/85	8.00	09/26/80-11/16/80	11.00
12/20/91-07/02/92	3.50	11/21/84-12/21/84	8.50	07/28/80-09/25/80	10.00
11/06/91-12/20/91	4.50	04/09/84-11/20/84	9.00	06/13/80-07/27/80	11.00
09/13/91-11/06/91	5.00	12/15/82-04/08/84	8.50	05/30/80-06/12/80	12.00
04/30/91-09/12/91	5.50	11/22/82-12/14/82	9.00	02/15/80-05/29/80	13.00
02/01/91-04/30/91	6.00	10/12/82-11/21/82	9.50	10/08/79-02/14/80	12.00
12/19/90-02/01/91	6.50	08/27/82-10/11/82	10.00	09/19/79-10/07/79	11.00
02/24/89-12/17/90	7.00	08/16/82-08/26/82	10.50	08/17/79-09/18/79	10.50
08/09/88-02/23/89	6.50	08/02/82-08/15/82	11.00	07/20/79-08/16/79	10.00
09/04/87-08/09/88	6.00	07/20/82-08/01/82	11.50	11/01/78-07/19/79	9.50
08/21/86-09/03/87	5.50	12/04/81-07/19/82	12.00	10/16/78-10/30/78	8.50
07/11/86-08/20/86	6.00	11/02/81-12/03/81	13.00	09/22/78-10/15/78	8.00
04/21/86-07/10/86	6.50	10/13/81-11/01/81	14.00	08/21/78-09/21/78	7.75
03/07/86-04/18/86	7.00	12/05/80-05/04/81	13.00	07/03/78-08/20/78	7.25
05/20/85-03/06/86	7.50	11/17/80-12/04/80	12.00	05/11/78-07/02/78	7.00

Index

A

Agricultural
  prices, 162
  workers, 178
Auction
  see U.S. Treasury
  sizes, 236-237
Automobile debt, 35, 36
Automotive dealers, 168
Average hourly earnings, 56, 71

B

Balanced Budget Act, 76
Bank Lending Survey, 200-201
Bargaining status, 69
Baseline outlook, 76
BEA, *see* Bureau of Economic
  Analysis
Benefits, *see* Hours-related, Em-
  ployer-paid, Legally, Retire-
  ment
Bill(s)
  see Cash
  passes, 214
BLS, *see* Bureau of Labor Statistics
Bonuses, 68, 71
  payments, 153
Borrowed reserves, 208, 225
Borrowings
  see Federal funds
  number, 228-229
BOS, *see* Business Outlook Survey
Budget
  see Congressional, Federal, Off-
    budget, On-budget

deficits, *see* Federal
  Enforcement Act of 1990, 76
  Resolution, 76
  surplus, 73
  terms, 76
Building(s)
  see Nonresidential, Residential
  permits, 99-103
  data analysis, 100-103
Bureau of Economic Analysis
  (BEA), 13, 14, 123, 153, 168
Bureau of Labor Statistics (BLS),
  40, 55, 57, 59, 64, 105, 160,
  166, 177
Business
  cycle, 4, 6, 12, 14, 24, 31, 45, 60,
    97, 103, 110, 115, 118, 122,
    124, 131-132, 138, 139, 165
  see U.S.
  contractions, 82
  incorporations, 59
  inventories, 11-15
  data analysis, 12-15
  sales, 11-15
  data analysis, 12-15
  service employee, 61
Business Outlook Survey (BOS),
  147-148

C

Capacity constraints, 126
Capacity utilization, 50, 105-113
  data, 105
  data analysis, 107-112
  definition, 108